The Complete Instant Pot Cookbook

Top 101 Delicious And Easy Instant Pot Recipes With 2 Weeks Meal Plan To Reduce Overweight, Be More Healthier and Have A Better Lifestyle

By Angela Ellgen

"Table of Contents"

About the book

Ever had a problem finding recipes for an instant pot? Or do you have one in your house, sitting in a corner just because you don't know how to operate it? Clueless of how its functionality can help you in your everyday kitchen life? If so, then I'm proud to tell you that you just bought the right book!

Meticulously written after countless hours of experience and disasters in the kitchen, this book has been designed to help you learn all about the basics of an instant pot, including its functionality, advantages and its disadvantages. On completion of this book, it is rest assured that you will be able to operate this multi-faceted gadget at ease in your own convenience. Also in the book, I've included 101 delicious, quick and easy recipes for an instant pot, so right away, go into your kitchen and start testing them out today!

In appreciation, I thank you for buying this book and I hope you will enjoy reading it till the end, because your support is what motivates me to being a more better writer!

<u>About the author</u>

The author of this book and the subsequent ones to come, Angela Ellgen has worked for a long time as a writer, and has finally transitioned into becoming a seasoned book publisher. His works are carried out under the whims of in-depth researches, to ensure that everything he writes is reliable,factual and meaningful. To spice things up a bit, he always strives to convey information in a exciting and engaging way, without losing the quality of the information itself.

However, the greatest distinguishing feature about Angela Ellgen is his passion towards helping people, which you'll get to see as you go deeper in this book. And this very feature is sacrosanct because, passion is the main driving force to getting things done, without passion there will certainly be no accomplishments of any magnitude.So, with him being a writer with passion towards helping people, Angela Ellgen gives his all through his books, to help his readers get the best out of what they've bought and impact their lives positively . A writer by day and a reader by night, Angela Ellgen beyond all reasonable doubts, is certainly a star that will soon shine!

Chapter 1

The Instant Pot

On reading this first chapter, we will discuss what an instant pot is, how it works, and why it is better than other pots and cookers. So let the journey begin!

The basic definition of an Instant Pot:

An Instant Pot is a type of multi-cooker that can do the job of seven different kitchen appliances, which include pot warmer, browning the pan, yogurt maker, steamer, rice cooker, pressure cooker and last but not the least, the slow cooker. Sounds too good to be true, right? Well, we will get to that find out.

When it first came into the market, people marveled at its magnificence and impressiveness, particularly because it was one of the most overpriced tool in the market those days, 5 years later, and it is now one of the most commonly used and loved multi-functional machine by everyone. Why? Because it encompasses a handful of kitchen appliances into one single unit, which can send even mildly experienced cooks into fits of passion.

The primary reason to this is that, the machine can potentially send electric pressure cookers into extinction, as it is one of the fastest growing appliances in the kitchen sector, with the sales getting doubled and even tripled in the last few years. The product claims that it can make food faster, in a healthier way as well. So who wants a cooker now?

Speaking of pacy cooking, I guess its high time we ventured into how the Instant Pot actually works, and why it is getting so famous that, you probably hear its name from each and every chef and professional's mouth these days.

The intricate functionality of the Instant Pot:

Want to whip up some nutritious meals for yourself and your family? Understand the basic workings here first!

Instant Pots come in different variants, the various functions and features inclusive, but the basic utility of the machine is always the same. Instead of wasting time pondering on the functionality of each part of the machine, without any further ado, lets hit the nail on the head!

Don't get fazed by the looks of it!

You read that right. Everyone who sees the Instant Pot for the first time feels overwhelmed by the increasingly large amount of functions, buttons and settings. Regarding this, you don't need to worry as it is very easy to use and operate once you have read the manual thoroughly, which is one of the reason why it is loved so much all over the world. In addition,it is intuitive and even the greatest professionals have accepted defeat for not getting head over heels on its great results and simple nature!

Let me give you a little hint here, if you have ever used a pressure, rice or slow cooker, even once, then you are already halfway up to learning the full advance functionality of the Instant Pot, as it is nothing more than a pressure cooker that works on electricity, but just with some additional boatload of features!

Experiment on those pre-programmed functions!

If you are new to the use of the electric pressure cooker jazz, you'll most definitely be under a lot of tension! (Here is what I did). However, keeping in mind the large targeted audience, the manufacturers of the Instant Pot were kind enough to add a whole bunch of pre-programmed functional buttons. Now the good thing about this buttons is that, unlike that of the 90's, they do not breakdown after a week's usage or easily.

The Instant Pot's pre-programmed settings are properly constructed, which include the basics, all the way to the intricate work, from soups, poultry, rice to beef and stews, all aimed at a single button click cooking style, for your favorite food. That being said, the question still remains, is it good enough?

Well, given that the functions are pre-programmed, one may not have that much of a choice if he/she wants to cook something different from their everyday routine. However, the individual can easily salvage the situation by choosing his/her settings manually. It's a bummer, but that's the only way it will work if you want it to.But in essence,the fact that it necessitates a smooth, pacy and qualitative style of cooking should never be taken out of the picture

Go bulky if you want to!

The best thing, in my opinion, about the Instant Pot is that whether you cook a whole kilogram of rice or just 2 servings, it always takes a maximum of 10 minutes precisely. Sounds crazy, right? But how is that possible one may ask? Well, the pressure power in which the Instant Pot applies to every ingredient is always the same, invariably making the cooking of foods in large quantities effective, while saving time and energy at the same time, because realistically, nobody would want to cook a meal twice if he/she is presented with an opportunity to cook and store them once.

On the other hand, the Instant Pot is a magical product that frankly, has changed my life completely. Nowadays, I don't have to go through the stress of making the same food twice, as I can easily prepare double the quantity together, thereafter split it into halves and preserve it for the night using the fridge. Then when the night comes, I can simply take it out, heat it, and eat it with freshly steamed vegetables straight from the Instant Pot. In fact, it is a very handy tool, if you know how to use it properly.

Life hack: You can reheat your leftovers

You can take it as a nifty life hack, but to be completely honest with you, it works really well! This hack uses the steam function, which is the most aggressive setting in the Instant Pots of this generation. It dials the Instant Pot straight to its full heat and pressure, designed to work for only 5-10 minutes. It is usually used to steam vegetables, to clean them from harmful germs and bacteria.

Also, you can incinerate your leftovers and frozen meals, by just pouring 1 cup of water in the Instant Pot, letting the moisture build up, and then putting the leftovers in the Instant Pot. Moreover, there are a few tricks to this, if you are defrosting an already packaged meal, remove the plastic rack before you bring it into the pressure, as the food can get ruined by the plastic, and if you are using any frozen leftovers, ensure that you put the block in a casserole dish on the rack, before putting it in the Instant Pot. Considering the time frame, smaller quantities can take less than 3 minutes, while the larger ones and the whole pre-packaged meals can take up 7 to 10 minutes.

Seamlessly switch if you want to!

All Instant Pot models currently being sold, are now vested with the capacity of switching from one mode to the other simultaneously, and if you think about it carefully, that is a great deal of stress lifted off your shoulders. Remember the time when you had to run around the kitchen handling the heating, simmering, cooking and boiling all at once? Well, with the Instant Pot, the whole above mentioned processes usually become s a piece of cake!

You can adjust the timer to when you want the Instant Pot to change the modes, or do it manually yourself. For example, you can heat an onions in the pot initially, then instantly switch to the pressure cooker and add the beef to continue the recipe without much effort. In a nutshell, it is a lifesaver, as you can increase your productivity in the time you saved, and reduce the number of dishes you will have to wash.

The comparative showdown of the Instant Pot:

As the popular saying goes, beauty is in the eyes of the beholder, so is it also applicable in choosing appliances, because the true importance and value of any machine can only be derived if it is compared to its counterpart. In the case of the Instant Pot, we will be comparing it with the Cuisinart CPC-600, which you can say is the literal cousin to the Instant Pot family. The Cuisinart CPC-600 is made by a different, but well-renowned manufacturer, so comparing it with the Instant Pot would be meaningless, rather, we will be comparing each part of the Instant Pot with its competitor to see if the Instant Pot, actually has more edge over others.

Appearance

The appearance of both the electric pressure and slow cookers are almost the same, which is one of the main reasons why I said that it is really similar. The interior part of both machines are made of stainless steel, really hard, durable, and to crown it all,resistance to dents. However, the Instant Pot looks too sophisticated as a whole, particularly because of its buttons layout and interface, making it a win for the Instant Pot in this aspect. This very statement, takes us to the next step of this comparative analysis, which is...

Functionality

The first impression that most people often do have when looking at an Instant Pot, is always that it looks a lot better than the Cuisinart in terms of functionality, because it has a larger array of buttons, functional keys and indicators,. Although some people still prefer the minimalistic design of the Cuisinart as well, however, larger quantity is not always better, because the Instant Pot's settings can take a while to get used to, as the buttons may make it hard to navigate and operate. The Cuisinart is simpler in this regard, and wins the ease of use part of the machine.

For example, when I first unpacked my Instant Pot out of the box, I tried to make something from it. I have forgotten what it was, but I can remeber deliberately searching the buttons for the one I wanted. I didn't want soup or rice, beans or poultry, and in the end, I finally figured out that the 'manual' button was the one I had to use. I blamed myself for that, because I didn't even read the manual before trying it out. So in brief, always read the manual first!

One honorable mention to this fact is that, the Instant Pot makes a small beep on each button press, which helps in deciphering if you pressed the right button on not. While the Instant Pot beats the Cuisinart in this respect, the Cuisinart has many indicators as well, making the functionality regards between both machines to end in a tie.

Timers

Timing is a sacrosanct key in cooking, which is why I decided to add this to the comparison as well, in regards to the fact that timers are an essential factor in any cooking machine. Whenever you press a button to activate a mode, the Instant Pot starts directly at 30 minutes, and if you want to cook something for only 2-3 minutes, you're going to waste a lot of time pressing the same 'less' button 27 times. The Cuisinart's timer, however starts at one, so it definitely saves a lot of hassle.

Also, the Instant Pot automatically starts after one minute if you don't modify the settings or press start, which is pretty helpful, but at the same time, distressing for some. Stressful because, supposing that you wanted to make a food in the morning, then you filled the Instant Pot up in the night, and turned all the settings on, to let it rest for the night so you can just press start when you wake up, it would be cumbersome because this setting of the Instant Pot, makes it a pain to do that, and the worst part is that you can't disable it, meaning that you're going to be stuck with this until the next generation of the machine comes out.

Size

This factor can easily be guessed in a single glance of both machines placed side by side. The Instant Pot is a whole lot bulkier than the Cuisinart, maybe because of the extra features and the stainless steel interior, but who knows? The handles might just be another factor that contributes to its bulkiness, which makes it tedious, carrying it along if you are an avid traveler or tourist. And if you are one, the main question should be "Why are you carrying an electric pressure cooker around the world?"

In addition, the Cuisinart's power cord is lighter and removable, while that of the Instant Pot is permanent, more flexible and durable,invariably meaning that the Instant Pot takes the ball out of the park for this one.

Also, both cookers have the same dimensions and capacities, which is, 6 quartz. But in my total experience, the Instant Pot's storage seems a whole lot more than the Cuisinart. Although it isn't proven, it's just a thought I have always had while comparing both of them.

Features

I always save the best for the last, and in this comparison, the feature section is the most important for kitchen appliances of this type. The Cuisinart and Instant Pot share a lot of functions, including the slow cooker, the rice cooker, the pressure cooker, the steamer and the warmer. However, the main feature that is only exclusive to the Instant Pot is the heat mode, which is often tagged as the browning mode in the Cuisinart. The Instant Pot's sauté mode makes the machine go wild, hitting it up to the highest pressure so you can roast, defrost and heat all the food you want in the least amount of time.

The unique yogurt feature is also exclusive to the Instant Pot, and sounds pretty intriguing. In as much as I haven't tried it myself, I am certain that it is a promising feature. So, in a nutshell, the Instant Pot wins the final round of our comparative analysis, invariably taking us to our grand conclusion.

Is It Really worth it?

Irrespective of how renowned, famous and great the machine is, it always balls down to this single question. Is it really worth my purchase? Well, in order to arrive at an answer to this question, we will firstly have to discuss each aspect of the machine and its merits.

It is great as a slow cooker

Unlike most slow cookers that only have a crock for heating, the Instant Pot has a small inner stainless steel pot that is heated by the outer device itself. Skeptically,some people may think that the food will easily stick to the interior surface, but in my experience, it has never happened before. The coils used for heating the Instant Pot are pretty well placed and regulated to avoid burning and overheating.

However, the only complaint that many people levy on it is that, the heat settings are pretty limited. Adding that, the low setting isn't enough to get a large amount of soup heated in a small amount of time, while the high one is not as high as it should be in terms of heating, meaning it takes more time than it should to heat a simple dish.

The Sauté mode has the most value

The sauté mode, in my opinion, offers the highest value in the entire tool-set that the machine provides. It can be used for a plethora of tasks, ranging from heating, defrosting, and also sautéing. With this feature present in the Instant Pot, you won't need to make your pan dirty just to heat some measly onion or peppers. Personally, the sauté feature is the only feature I use almost every time ,that I turn on the Instant Pot.

The pressure cooker is very speedy

In my opinion, this is the coolest feature present in an Instant Pot. The cooker is designed to calculate the amount of food present in the pot and the time taken to cook it, so that it can fully optimize itself for the task coming ahead. Another good thing is that the amount of food, does not affect the pressure cooker in the least bit.

If it takes 20 minutes to dry a rice, it will always take 20 minutes. But as they say, to every strength comes a weakness, and in this case, here are the flaws.

The pot is too small for canning

The pot is okay if you want to cook a one or two-time meal, but if you are planning to carryout some pressure canning, you're better off doing it with a large pressure cooker, because it will take a lot of time, and will only give you a maximum of 3 medium sized jars. However, if you want to play around with the pressure and sizes of the jars, maybe it will work out, and if it does, ring me up so I'll do that to!

You'll need to buy a separate lid if you are looking for a long term use

That's right, but why? The default lid that comes out of the box is colored, and is extremely awkward if you are planning to use it as a slow cooker. The lid does not allow you to see the inner part of the pot, and given that slow cooking is all about the pressure, you can't open the lid and see your meal with your very own eyes. So, if you are thinking of using it for a long time as a pressure or slow cooker, you should buy the transparent, tampered lid. It is great and cheap, but to me,it feels like the tampered lid should have been the default one instead of the current one. So, cutting the long story short, the total cost of the Instant Pot will be $20 higher than the normal retail price, if you count the lid.

It is an electric device, and you know what that means...

Being an electrical device,it won't last as long as a regular pressure or slow cooker. There is often a saying that posits that, the more complex the machine is, the higher the chances are that it will break down easily, and so in addressing the issue of the Instant Pot,the case is no different as its durability depends solely on your usage. In respect to that, you'll need to clean it once a week, and manually clean the inner part of the machine, which can be pretty tough if you cooked something that involved liquids before cleaning it.

Is it worth it?

So again, the bottom line is, is it really worth it? Well here is the answer:

"If you are a newly married couple looking to equip your kitchen, the Instant Pot is the best as it is a seven in one machine. However, if you are a seasoned chef or cook, you may need to reconsider, as it is of no use if you already have all it offers. Still, if you are planning to reduce your arsenal to the least amount of tools, you should get it, but remember, it won't last you for a long time as your old' trusty frying pan would."

Chapter 2

Diets:

Of course, what would a cookbook be if it doesn't have a chapter dedicated for diets? In this small but useful chapter, we will look at the basic definition of a diet, the different types of diets, and the perfect meal plan for an Instant Pot owner, so let's delve right in!

The basic definition of a diet:

What is a diet? Is it a lifestyle? Or simply just foods categorized into groups? Well, the word diet means the food consumed by any individual. It is often said in a way that implies the intake of nutrients. However, you mustn't confuse it with dieting, as dieting is a practice of reduce excess fat and weight through the use of diets(food).

Every human being's diet is different, particularly because of his or her personal tastes, ethical limitations, and culture. For example, Indians have a diet that mostly consists of spices and different types of meat, while the Koreans usually have a large intake of different vegetables on a daily basis. Religions also plays a major role in a person's diet, for example, Buddhists are generally vegetarians, while Hindus are not. You may have heard the term 'Halal' in your life at least once, right? Well,this term means food that are permitted for the Muslims to eat. So, what are we saying here? Diets can vary for each human being due to an uncountable set of reasons.

Diets are one of the biggest determinant factors for a person's good health, as a healthy diet is a necessity for anyone who wishes to maintain a healthy lifestyle. Almost all health agencies around the world encourage people to maintain a normal diet consisting of just the right amount of nutrients and sugar. They do that by limiting the consumption of foods that are dense in terms of energy, drinks that are full of sugar, plants, processed meat, and of course, alcohol.

There are different types of diets, which will be the next thing we will discuss in this chapter. They are for everyone, those who are obese, those who are too thin, weak, and even those that want to maintain the perfect equilibrium of both health status. They are usually practiced for many months before the final result is achieved, and some are really intense, so what are we waiting for? Let's jump right into the details of each!

Types of diets:

Before we head into the details, let us look at a little introduction to the types of diets, if you don't want to read, feel free to skip!

There are a thousand different types of diets in this current generation. Some are designed for the purpose of losing weight, while others are made for gaining it, some are for lowering cholesterol, while others are made for increasing it. There is certainly a diet for everyone, so in order to keep the book short and precise, I have written 5 of the best diets for all types of people, so choose yours and start working today!

Ketogenic Diet

Being one of the most common diets in the world, the Ketogenic plan is well known for being a diet containing the lowest amount of carbohydrates, and here's how it works. Whenever you eat something that has a lot of carbs, your body will make it turn into glucose,thereafter uses the glucose as energy to carry out its tasks. Since only glucose is used, the fats are left unused and as a result piles up. So, the Ketogenic diet aims at lowering the intake of carbohydrates, so that the fat accumulated in the body will be used. In this diet, you should aim at eating foods like meat and vegetables while trying to avoid high carb foods like grains, fruits, potatoes, and sugar-based stuff.

Atkins Diet

The Atkins Diet is very similar to the Ketogenic Diet, and aims at reducing excess weight in the body. It started in 1972, and is one of the most widely regarded diets for weight loss. This diet consists of foods that have low carbs, but are high in fat. It is really effective because when people start adapting to this diet, their appetite goes a long way down, and in the end, they automatically end up eating less calories on a daily basis. In this diet, you should not eat recipes that have Grains (Wheat, Rice), Oils (Soybean Oil, Canola Oil), 'low-fat' foods, high-carb veggies (Carrots, Turnips), high-carb fruits (Bananas, Apples) etc. However, you should try your best to take stuffs like seeds, meat, eggs and full-fat dairy on a daily basis.

Paleo Diet

The Paleo Diet is the complete opposite of the two diets discussed earlier, as it aims at going back to the roots of humanity and encourages you to take nature's advantage, and eat all that it has to offer. In other words, in this diet, you should only opt for things like nuts, fish, veggies, fruits, and seeds. In a nutshell, anything that didn't exist in the caveman times can neither be in your plate, nor in your stomach, so the marshmallows and candies have to go! Why is this diet even recommended by experts? Because instead of worrying about the calories and partitioned portions of food most diets tell you, you'll only be focusing only on eating what is right for you, without worrying about anything else!

Dash Diet

This diet is really different from the ones we've discussed earlier, as it mostly encourages people to eat a variety of foods that are made to prevent or treat hypertension, that is, high blood pressure. It is aimed at reducing the amount of excess sodium in the body that mostly results in the increase of systolic blood pressure. After following just the 2 weeks of this diet plan, you will notice a significant decrease in blood pressure to over 14 points.   So if you are a heart patient, try it out today, you won't regret any moment of doing it!

Vegetarian Diet

Of course, it would be pointless writing a chapter on diets, if it didn't include one of the most well-known, commonly practiced diets in the world, that's right; I'm talking about the vegetarian diet. Relying on an all-vegetable diet may actually be a better way to live life, as studies show that vegetarians have a lesser chance of having cancer, mental health issues and allergies as opposed to other people. However, studies also show that vegetarians are less healthy due to their rejection towards meat, which has a high amount of proteins. So whatever the case maybe, it's all your choice!

A perfect 2-week diet plan:

This section is carefully crafted after looking at all the different diets we've discussed above, and features a diet plan with all the limitations and prevented foods of each diet, except the vegetarian diet, as it doesn't allow for the intake of meat. Also, all of the dishes can be cooked easily in an Instant Pot, so if you want a plan that is an all-rounder for all sorts of diets, this is certainly the plan for you!

Here's how it goes:

Week 1:

Day 1:

    Breakfast: Brown Butter Oatmeal

    Lunch: Turkey and White Bean Chili

    Dinner: BBQ Lentils over Baked Potato Wedges

Day 2:

    Breakfast: Classical Irish Oatmeal

    Lunch: Salsa Chicken

    Dinner: BBQ Chicken Drumsticks

Day 3:

    Breakfast: Apple and Cinnamon Oatmeal

    Lunch: Kashmiri Potato Curry

    Dinner: Middle Eastern Millet Pilaf

Day 4:

    Breakfast: Crème Brulee

    Lunch: Cola Chicken Wings

    Dinner: Seafood Stew

Day 5:

    Breakfast: Hard-Boiled Eggs

    Lunch: Pasta Caprese

    Dinner: Instant Mexi-Cali Rice

Day 6:

    Breakfast: Smokey Sweet Potato Mash

Lunch: Instant Potatouille

Dinner: Indian Style Apricot Chicken

Day 7:

Breakfast: Maple French Toast Casserole

Lunch: Lemon-sage Spaghetti Squash

Dinner: Mergherita Chicken with Sundried Tomato Sauce

Week 2:

Day 1:

Breakfast: Easy Potato Beans

Lunch: Buffalo Hot Wings

Dinner: Cauliflower Potato Curry

Day 2:

Breakfast: Purple Yam Barley Porridge

Lunch: Italian Cannellini and Mint Salad

Dinner: Coconut Fish Curry

Day 3:

Breakfast: Peaches and Cream Oatmeal

Lunch: Spicy Sous-Vide Tempeh

Dinner: Couscous and Vegetable Medley

Day 4:

Breakfast: Slow-Cook Oatmeal with Apples

Lunch: New England Clam Chowder

Dinner: Teriyaki Chicken and Rice

Day 5:

Breakfast: Brown Butter Oatmeal

Lunch: Honey Garlic Chicken Lettuce Wraps

Dinner: Shrimp and Grits

Day 6:

Breakfast: Peaches and Cream Oatmeal

Lunch: Pine Nuts Honey Mousse

Dinner: Smokey Beat Black Eyed Peas

Day 7:

Breakfast: Three minute Oats

Lunch: Chickpea Curry

Dinner: Lemon and Herb Chicken

Chapter 3

101 Recipes for the Instant Pot:

Since this is a cookbook, it wouldn't be nice if we do not include the ones for the Instant Pot, right? The recipes below are written by the best of the best, so you can treat this compilation of 101 recipes on the same caliber of your favorite cooking show. The recipes are divided into 5 categories, which include Breakfast, Dessert, Poultry, Vegan, and last but not the least, others (like rice, pastas, soups and stews). So without wasting time, let's jump right into it!

Breakfast:

Recipe # 1: Brown Butter Oatmeal:

Serves: 4-6 people

Preparation time: 5 minutes

Cooking Time: 17 minutes

Ingredients:

1. 2 tablespoons of unsalted butter
2. 1 ½ cups of oats, steel cut
3. 4 ½ cups of warm water
4. ½ teaspoon of salt, can change according to taste
5. Brown sugar, for serving

6. Heavy Cream, for serving

Directions:

1. Press the sauté mode on your Instant Pot, and melt the butter. Add the oats into the pot and heat it for 5 minutes whilst still stirring until the oats are lightly roasted.
2. Add the water, salt and continue stirring. Make sure that all the ingredients are submerged into the water. If not, then add more.
3. Close the lid and adjust the 'Steam release' to 'sealing'. Change the cooking mode to 'Porridge' and cook it for 12 minutes at a high pressure.
4. When the cooking stops, let the pressure release naturally, and after 10 minutes, set the 'Steam Release' back to 'venting' to remove the remaining steam.
5. Take the oatmeal out of the pot and ladle it into a bowl. Serve it with the brown sugar and heavy cream. You can also try variations with various other ingredients, like peanut butter, sesame soy and blueberry almond. Enjoy!

Recipe # 2: Apple and Cinnamon Oatmeal:

Serves: 4 people

Preparation time: 5 minutes

Cooking Time: 9 minutes

Ingredients:

1. 3 tablespoons of regular butter
2. 1 cup of steel cut oats
3. 2 ½ cups of water
4. 1 large apple, chopped, cored and peeled. More to be needed for garnishing
5. 1 tablespoon of brown sugar, for serving
6. 1 teaspoon of cinnamon

7. ½ teaspoon of salt, more or less depending on your taste

Directions:

1. Select the sauté function of the Instant Pot and let it preheat. When the display indicator reads hot, add the butter and oats, and cook for 2 minutes.
2. Add the water, chopped apple, brown sugar, salt and cinnamon and stir well.
3. Secure the lid, set the setting to 'manual' and cook at high pressure for 7-9 minutes, depending on the amount of thickness you want.
4. Once the cooking is complete, let the steam release itself, and after 10 minutes, release the remaining steam by setting the 'Steam Release' setting to 'venting'.
5. Serve the oatmeal with brown sugar and nicely topped fresh apple. Enjoy!

Recipe # 3: Easy-to-make Vanilla Yogurt

Serves: 6 people

Preparation time: 10 minutes

Cooking Time: 10 hours, 15 minutes

Ingredients:

1. 4 cups of milk, 2% fat
2. 100 grams' vanilla yogurt, or a small container equivalent
3. 1 tablespoons of sugar
4. 4 cups of water

Directions:

1. Boil the milk on a high heat using a non-stick pot, or through the sauté option on the Instant Pot.
2. Let the milk cool at the room temperature.

3. After the milk has cooled down, add the yogurt, sugar and divide the mix into 4 different cups. If you used the Instant Pot in this step, clean it for the next one).

4. Add the water to the 4 cup mark in the Instant Pot and put all the four cups in the pot again. This is to ensure that the water level is equal to the amount of milk.

5. Secure the lid and choose the 'Keep warm' function for 15 minutes.

6. Let the pot rest in the warm heat for 10 hours. Do not open the lid, or all will go to waste.

7. After 10 hours has elapsed, take the yogurt out, cover it with a plastic wrap and let it chill for 2-3 hours before serving. Enjoy!

Recipe # 4: Classical Irish Oatmeal:

Serves: 4-6 people

Preparation time: 15 minutes

Cooking Time: 13 minutes

Ingredients:

1. ½ teaspoon of salt
2. 2 tablespoons of butter
3. 1 cup of steel-cut oats
4. 3 cups of water
5. ½ teaspoon of grounded cinnamon
6. ½ teaspoon of salt
7. ¼ cup of half-and-half, a common product found at dairy stores.
8. ¼ brown sugar
9. 1 cup of strawberries, for berry compote
10. 6 ounces of blackberries, for berry compote
11. 6 ounces of blueberries, for berry compote

12. 1 tablespoons of water, for berry compote
13. 3 tablespoons of sugar, granulated, for berry compote

Directions:

To make oatmeal:

1. Select the sauté function on the Instant Pot, and melt the butter. Add the oats and cook for 5 minutes while still stirring continuously.
2. Add the water, cinnamon, salt, and cook for 1 minute.
3. Close the lid, and cook at a high pressure for 13 minutes. Don't forget to set the 'Steam release' to 'Sealing'.
4. While the oatmeal is cooking, it would be the best time to make the berry compote. If you want to, you can, but you can also leave it for the end, as it is optional.
5. When the cooking is complete, naturally let the steam release and after 10 minutes, release the remaining pressure. Stir the oat until it is smooth.
6. Add half brown sugar, and stir till there are no lumps and the mix is perfectly blended.
7. Serve with Berry Compote. If you want the porridge to be thicker, cook the oatmeal for 2-3 minutes more at the sauté mode.

To make the Compote:

1. Mix the strawberries, blackberries, blueberries, water, sugar in a saucepan and simmer it using a medium heat.
2. Cook it for 8 to 9 minutes or until the berries are soft enough. Thereafter, serve it with the Oatmeal. Enjoy!

Recipe # 5: Peaches and Cream Oatmeal:

Serves: 4 people

Prep Time: 5 minutes

Cooking Time: 3 minutes

Ingredients:

1. 3 cups of oats, any types to taste
2. 4 cups of warm water
3. 1 peach, finely chopped
4. 1 teaspoon of vanilla
5. 2 tablespoons of flax meal, optional
6. 1/2 cup of Almonds, chopped into small pieces, optional
7. Milk, optional. Can also use cream if desired.
8. Maple Syrup, for additional taste, optional

Directions:

1. Add the rolled oats, peaches, vanilla and water into the Instant Pot. Adjust the mode to 'porridge' and cook at a high pressure for 3 minutes.
2. When finished, allow the heat and pressure to manually release itself, then after 10 minutes, remove the remaining by doing a quick pressure release.
3. Divide the porridge between 3 to 4 bowls, and serve it with the optional ingredients stated in the list above. Enjoy!

Recipe # 6: Purple Yam Barley Porridge:

Serves: 12 people

Prep Time: 10 minutes

Cooking Time: 45 minutes

Ingredients:

1. 3 tablespoons of pot barley
2. 3 tablespoons of pearl barley
3. 3 tablespoons of buckwheat

4. 3 tablespoons of black eye beans
5. 3 tablespoons of glutinous rice
6. 3 tablespoons of black glutinous rice
7. 3 tablespoons of Romano beans
8. 3 tablespoons of red beans
9. 3 tablespoons of brown rice
10. 1 purple yam, about 300 gms
11. 1/6 teaspoon of baking soda, optional

Directions:

1. Clean the purple yam, remove the skin and cut it into 1 centimeter cubes. Wash the barley, rice and beans as well.
2. Put the yam, rice, barley, beans and baking soda into the Instant Pot and add the water up to the 8 cups mark in the inner pot.
3. Secure the lid and set the mode to 'Manual'. Let the mix cook for 45 minutes.
4. When the time is up, let the pot sit for 10 minutes, then release the pressure. Serve and enjoy!

Recipe # 7: Maple French Toast Casserole:

Serves: 8 people

Prep Time: 8 minutes

Cooking Time: 1 hour, 30 minutes

Ingredients:

1. Cooking Spray, so that the ingredients don't stick in the Instant Pot.
2. 12 slices of sandwich bread cut into small 1 inch pieces. Can also use gluten-free bread if desired
3. 4 eggs, lightly beaten
4. 1/2 cup of maple syrup

5. 1 teaspoon of cinnamon
6. 1/2 teaspoon of kosher salt
7. 1/4 teaspoon of nutmeg, grated
8. 1/8 teaspoon of cloves
9. 2 cups of milk, reduced fat 2%
10. 1 teaspoon of powdered sugar

Directions:

1. Coat the inner pot of the Instant pot with the cooking spray. And place the cubed bread in the pot.
2. Mix the eggs, cinnamon, cloves, salt, nutmeg, and maple syrup in a large bowl. Add the milk and whisk all the ingredients till they are well blended.
3. Transfer the mix on the bread into the Instant Pot with a spoon, and then gently press the mixture so that all bread pieces are coated.
4. Secure the lid of the pot, select the 'Slow Cook' mode and set the time to 90 minutes.
5. After the time is up, serve with a sprinkle of powdered sugar. Enjoy!

Recipe # 8: Pink Lady Applesauce:

Serves: 8 to 10 people

Prep Time: 15 minutes

Cooking Time: 25 minutes

Ingredients:

1. 12 apples
2. 1 cup ofwarm or cold water
3. 2 tablespoons of zesty lemon juice

Directions:

1. Cut the apples into quarters, and peel them if you desire to. Add them to the Instant Pot along with the water and lemon juice.
2. Secure the lid and set the mode to 'Manual', and cook for 5 minutes.
3. When the timer sounds, let the Instant Pot rest for 10 to 15 minutes, then take the sauce out. If you want a thicker texture, then use a blender till you reach the desired result.
4. Place the sauce in jars into the fridge, and re-heat it whenever you want to! Enjoy!

Recipe # 9: Soy Milk Yogurt:

Serves: 4 to 6 people

Prep Time: 15 minutes

Cooking Time: 14 hours

Ingredients:

1. 3/4 cup of powdered soy milk
2. 1 teaspoon of sugar
3. 2 1/2 cups of hot water
4. 3/4 teaspoon of agar powder
5. 1/4 teaspoon of probiotic or vegan culture

Directions:

1. Add the water, soy milk, sugar into a blender and blend at a high speed for 3 minutes.
2. Add the agar powder into the mix and blend it also for 30 more seconds. After blending, allow the soy milk to settle down for 2-5 minutes.
3. Once the soy milk has settled down, add the probiotic powder or vegan culture and WHISK (don't blend)

4. Place the mixture into the Instant Pot, select the 'Yogurt' mode and set the timer to 14 hours,then wait.
5. Once the time is up, take the yogurt out and let it sit in the refrigerator for 2 more hours. You can skip this if you want to use it immediately. Enjoy!

Recipe # 10: Slow-Cook Oatmeal with Apples:

Serves: 10 people

Prep Time: 3 minutes

Cooking Time: 6 hours

Ingredients:

1. 1 pound of apples, diced
2. 2 cups of steel cut oats
3. 7 cups of water
4. 1/2 cup of honey, or maple syrup for vegans
5. 1/2 teaspoon of salt
6. 1/2 teaspoon of all-spice, grounded
7. 1 can coconut of milk, light
8. toasted cashews, optional
9. more apples, for topping, optional

Directions:

1. Cover the inner pot of the Instant Pot with oil and add the first seven ingredients in the inner pot.
2. Secure the lid, set the mode to 'Slow Cook', adjust it to 'Less' and cook for 6 hours.
3. Stir well before serving and garnish with cashews and apples, if desired. Enjoy!

Recipe # 11: Three minute Oats:

Serves: 4 people

Prep Time: 2 minutes

Cooking Time: 3 minutes

Ingredients:

1. 2 cups of warm water
2. 1 cup of milk, can be dairy, almond variations
3. 1 cup of steel cut oats
4. 1/2 vanilla bean
5. a pinch of salt
6. 1/2 cup of raisins or any other dry fruit
7. 1 teaspoon of cinnamon, grounded
8. 1/4 cup of walnuts
9. 1/2 tablespoon of maple syrup
10. olive oil, optional
11. 1 cinnamon stick, optional

Directions:

1. Add the water, milk, oats, vanilla bean, salt, cinnamon stick, olive oil and 1/4 cup of raisins to the Instant Pot.
2. Secure the lid, set the mode to 'Manual' and cook for 3 minutes. When the time is up, let the pressure come down itself.
3. Open the pot to check if the oats are cooked properly, if not, secure the lid again and let it rest for 10 minutes.
4. Once the oats are cooked, remove the vanilla bean, cinnamon stick and set it aside.
5. Stir the cinnamon, walnuts and the remaining raisins and sweetener for taste. You can refrigerate leftovers for up to 4 days, so enjoy!

Dessert:

Recipe # 12: Basic Rice Pudding:

Serves: 4 people

Prep Time: 5 minutes

Cooking Time: 15 minutes

Ingredients:

1. 1 cup of fine rice
2. 1 teaspoon of butter
3. 2 cups of non fat milk
4. 3/4 cups of sugar
5. 1 cup of water
6. 2 egg yolks
7. 1/2 cup of half-and-half
8. 1 tablespoon of vanilla
9. 1 teaspoon of cinnamon, optional
10. 1/4 cup of raisins, optional

Directions:

1. Set the Instant Pot mode to 'sauté'. Melt the butter, and then add the rice. Cook it for about 3 minutes, until the edges of the rice become golden.
2. While the rice is cooking, whisk the milk, water, sugar and when the rice gets cooked, add them to the Instant Pot.
3. Set the mode to 'Manual' and cook at a high pressure for 10 minutes. After the time gets exhausted, let the pressure release itself, then do a quick release.
4. While the pressure is releasing, whisk the eggs, vanilla and the half-and-half.
5. Once you open the pot, add half a cup of the rice mixture into the egg mix, stirring constantly. Pour the resultant mixture back into the Instant Pot with the optional ingredients.
6. Set the mode back to 'sauté' and cook for 3 minutes while constantly stirring the mixture.

7. Then serve either warm or cold, according to your preference. Enjoy!

Recipe # 13: Quick Apple Pie Rice Pudding:

Serves: 4 people

Prep Time: 5 minutes

Cooking Time: 5 minutes

Ingredients:

1. 4 cups of rice, preferably grain brown
2. 4 cups of apples, finely chopped into small cubes
3. 2 cups of non-dairy, unsweetened milk
4. 1 tablespoon of Apple Pie Spice, or cinnamon, whichever you prefer
5. 1 tablespoon of Vanilla
6. 1/4 teaspoon of ground cardamom
7. 1 cup of golden raisins

Directions:

1. Place all the ingredients in the Instant Pot, and cook on a 'manual' mode for 5 minutes.
2. Once done, wait for the pressure to release itself slowly, and after 10 minutes, do a quick release.
3. Enjoy! Also, you can use this as a replacement for your usual oatmeal, and can serve it hot, cold or warm!

Recipe # 14: Carrot Pudding:

Serves: 4 people

Prep Time: 10 minutes

Cooking Time: 20 minutes

Ingredients:

1. 2 tablespoons of ghee, or vegan
2. 10 cups of carrots, grated and peeled
3. 1 cup of almond milk, unsweetened
4. 3/4 cup of sugar
5. 1 cup of almond meal
6. 2 teaspoons of cardamom powder
7. 2 tablespoons of raisins
8. 1/2 teaspoon of saffron
9. 2 tablespoon of pistachios, sliced

Directions:

1. Turn the Instant Pot on into the 'Sauté' mode, add the ghee and carrots. Cook for 2-3 minutes with the lid on.
2. Add the almond milk and close the lid, while making sure that the 'Pressure value' is set to 'sealing'.Thereafter set the Instant Pot to cook on 'Manual' and adjust to a high pressure for 5 minutes.
3. Quick release the pressure when the time is up, add the sugar, almond meal, raisins, saffron and cardamom powder. Mix all the ingredients well.
4. Turn the Instant Pot to 'Sauté' on a high heat again and cook for 5-7 minutes, until all the liquids are evaporated.
5. Garnish it with the sliced pistachios, serve and Enjoy!

Recipe # 15: Cheesecake Pops:

Serves: 6 people, 18 pops

Prep Time: 30 minutes

Cooking Time: 30 minutes

Ingredients:

1. 1/2 cup of sugar
2. 16 ounces' cream cheese, room temp.
3. 2 tablespoons of sour cream
4. 2 eggs
5. 1 teaspoon of vanilla extract
6. 1-pound of chocolate

Directions:

1. Using a mixing bowl, mix the cream cheese and sugar until it gets smooth. Blend in the sour cream ,vanilla and mix the eggs one at a time. Don't over mix tho.
2. Prepare a spring form the pan by coating it with non-stick spray. Transfer the batter prepared above into it.
3. Pour 1 cup of water into the Instant Pot, transfer the mixture and pan into the Instant Pot. Close the lid, select the 'High Pressure' and cook for 30 minutes. After the time has elapsed, use the quick release to remove the pressure.
4. Use a paper towel to soak up any pressure resultant water above the cheesecake, and remove the pan on a wire rack to cool. After it is cooled, refrigerate it for 4 hours or overnight while covering it with a plastic wrap.
5. After it is chilled, scoop the cake into small balls and insert a lollipop stick into each ball. Thereafter freeze it for 2 hours or more.
6. After the pops are frozen, dippen them into the melted chocolate. Shake off any excess, and refrigerate the pops until they are hard but easy to eat.

Recipe # 16: Cinnamon Raisin Bread Pudding:

Serves: 6 to 8 people

Prep Time: 25 minutes

Cooking Time: 35 minutes

Ingredients:

1. 4 to 5 cups of French Bread, cut to 1 inch cubes
2. 1 cup of raisins
3. 2 cups of milk
4. 2 eggs
5. 1 egg yolk
6. 1/4 cup of granulated sugar
7. 1/8 teaspoon of ground cinnamon
8. 1/8 teaspoon of ground nutmeg
9. 1 1/2 cup of water

Directions:

1. Spray a 7 inch round baking dish that fits in the Instant Pot with non-stick cooking spray. Mix the bread cubes and raisins in the dish, then distribute the raisins evenly.
2. Whisk the eggs, yolk, sugar, milk, nutmeg and cinnamon in a bowl until it is properly blended. Pour this mixture over the bread, and cover it with an aluminum foil. Thereafter, let it rest for 15 minutes.
3. Pour the water into the Instant Pot, place the baking dish inside and don't take off the foil.
4. Close the lid and cook for 35 minutes at the 'Manual' mode on a high pressure. When the cooking is complete, remove the pressure after 10 minutes.
5. Take the dish out, remove the foil, serve the pudding warm and enjoy!

Recipe # 17: Creamy Rice Pudding:

Serves: 8 people

Prep Time: 10 minutes

Cooking Time: 16 minutes

Ingredients:

1. 3/4 cup of sugar
2. 1/2 teaspoon of salt
3. 2 eggs
4. 5 cups of milk, 1% fat
5. 1 1/2 cups of Arborio or regular rice
6. 1 cup of half-and-half
7. 1 1/2 teaspoons of vanilla extract

Directions:

1. Mix the sugar, salt, rice and milk in the Instant Pot. Select the 'Sauté' mode and cook the contents uncovered till they are boiled. As soon as they start boiling, cover the lid.
2. Change the mode to 'Manual', adjust to a low pressure and cook for 16 minutes.
3. Whilst the rice is cooking, whisk the eggs, vanilla and the half-and-half. When the cooking is done, turn off the pressure cooker, and wait for 10 minutes before using the quick pressure release.
4. Add the egg mixture into the pot while stirring the rice, select the 'Sauté' mode and then cook it uncovered until the mixture boils.
5. Turn off the cooker,transfer the pudding into the bowls and serve immediately, or let them chill, your choice! Enjoy!

Recipe # 18: Crème Brulee:

Serves: 6 to 10 people

Prep Time: 35 minutes

Cooking Time: 15 minutes

Ingredients:

1. 2 cups of fresh cream
2. 5 tablespoons of white sugar
3. 6 egg yolks
4. 1 teaspoon of vanilla extract
5. 4 tablespoons of raw sugar, to be used for caramelizing

Directions:

1. Combine the egg yolks, sugar, cream and vanilla in a mixing bowl, then whisk until everything is combined properly, don't over mix tho.
2. Pour the mixture into the ramekins through a strainer, and cover them tightly in the foil. Put the ramekins into the Instant Pot, making sure they are vertically straight.
3. Cover the lid, and cook on the 'Manual' mode for 9 minutes. When the time is up, open the cooker using a natural release.
4. Take out the custards, and check by jiggling them. If they are almost solid in nature,it means they're OK, but if they feel watery, then cook for 5 more minutes.
5. Let the custards cool off for 30 minutes to an hour. Once they are cooled, put them in a refrigerator, and let them chill for 4 hours or overnight.
6. Before serving, sprinkle some raw sugar on top, then use a culinary torch or place them under the boiler for 5 minutes to caramelize. Enjoy!

Recipe # 19: One Step Arroz Pina Colada:

Serves: 6 to 10 people

Prep Time: 5 minutes

Cooking Time: 15 minutes

Ingredients:

1. 1 cup of Arborio rice
2. 1 cup of condensed milk, can add more for extra sweetness
3. 2/3 cup of pineapple juice
4. 1 ½ cups of water
5. 1 tablespoon of cinnamon
6. 1 cup of coconut milk, full fat

Directions:

1. Combine the rice and water in the Instant Pot, then cook at a low pressure for 12 minutes using either the 'rice' mode or the 'manual' mode.
2. When the cooking is dome, release the pressure quickly and add half of the coconut milk, all the condensed milk, the cinnamon and the pineapple juice. Thereafter, mix properly.
3. Let the mixture cool and absorb all the liquid. After it has thickened, add the remaining coconut milk to make the pudding thinner and Enjoy!

Recipe # 20: Pine Nuts Honey Mousse:

Serves: 6 to 8 people

Prep Time: 15 minutes

Cooking Time: 25 minutes

Ingredients:

1. 2 eggs
2. ½ cup of honey
3. 1 ¼ cup of coconut cream
4. 1 tablespoon of coconut oil
5. 1 ¼ cup of pine nuts
6. Chocolate Ganache, for topping

Directions:

1. Prepare a spring form pan by coating it with coconut oil, thereafter,line the bottom and sides with a parchment paper.
2. Put the eggs, honey and cream into a blender and mix until it gets completely smooth, then pour the mixture into the pan.
3. Pour one cup of water into the Instant Pot and place the pan inside. Close the lid and cook on a high pressure for 25 minutes using the 'Manual' mode.
4. Once the time is up, open the lid and take out the pan. Let it rest for 30 minutes or so. After that, invert the contents, take out the parchment paper, then put them again in the spring form pan, and let it refrigerate overnight.
5. If desired, top it with the Chocolate Ganache, or eat it without it. Enjoy!

Recipe # 21: Pressure Cooker Baked Apples:

Serves: 6 apples

Prep Time: 5 minutes

Cooking Time: 20 minutes

Ingredients:

1. 6 apples, cored
2. ¼ cup of raisins
3. 1 cup of red wine
4. ½ cup of sugar
5. 1 teaspoon of cinnamon

Directions:

1. Add the apples into the Instant Pot, and then sprinkle the raisins, sugar and cinnamon on top of it. Finally, add the red wine.
2. Cover the lid and cook on a high pressure for 10 minutes. When the time is up, let the pressure naturally release itself.
3. After the pressure has been released, serve it in a small bowl with lots of cooking liquid. Enjoy!

Recipe # 22: Red Wine Poached Pears:

Serves: 6 people

Prep Time: 5 minutes

Cooking Time: 10 minutes

Ingredients:

1. 6 pears, peeled
2. 1 bottle of red wine
3. 1 bay leaf
4. 1 stick of cinnamon
5. 4 cloves
6. 1-piece of ginger, fresh
7. 1 1/3 cups of sugar

Directions:

1. Pour the wine, bay leaf, cloves, ginger, sugar, cinnamon and pears into the Instant Pot.
2. Cover the lid and cook on a high pressure for 9 minutes using the 'Manual' mode. When the time is up, use the quick pressure release.
3. Take the pears out and cook the remaining liquid on the 'Sauté' mode until the volume of the liquid is reduced to at least half.
4. Take the liquid out, and pour it on the pears using a large bowl. Garnish it with preferred herbs and serve at a room temperature or chilled. Enjoy!

Poultry:

Recipe # 23: BBQ Chicken Drumsticks:

Serves: 4 to 6 people

Prep Time: 5 minutes

Cooking Time: 25 minutes

Ingredients:

1. 4-10 chicken drumsticks
2. 4 ½ teaspoons of black pepper,
3. ¼ cup of sweet paprika
4. 1 tablespoon of salt
5. 1 ½ teaspoons of garlic powder
6. 1 ½ teaspoons of regular salt
7. 1 ½ teaspoons of cayenne pepper
8. 1 ½ teaspoons of dry mustard
9. 1 ½ teaspoons of ground cumin

Directions:

1. Add ¾ of cup of water into the Instant Pot, place the chicken drumsticks inside it, and cook it for 20 minutes using the 'Poultry' mode.
2. Preheat the oven and line a cookie sheet with some parchment paper. When the timer for the Instant Pot beeps open the lid and take out the drumsticks.
3. Coat the drumsticks with the BBQ rub evenly, and line them on the cookie sheet. Broil the drumsticks for 2 minutes per side, but be careful not to burn them.
4. Serve immediately. Enjoy!

Recipe # 24: Chicken Lazone:

Serves: 6 people

Prep Time: 10 minutes

Cooking Time: 3 minutes

Ingredients:

1. 2 teaspoons of garlic powder
2. 1 teaspoon of chili powder
3. 1 teaspoon of paprika
4. 1 teaspoon of onion powder
5. 1/2 teaspoon of pepper
6. 1 teaspoon of salt
7. 2 tablespoons of butter
8. 2-pound of tender chicken
9. 2 tablespoons of oil
10. 2 tablespoons of cornstarch
11. 1/2 cup of chicken broth
12. 2 cups of heavy cream
13. 2 tablespoons of water
14. 2 tablespoons of parsley, finely chopped
15. 12 ounces' of spaghetti, cooked through the package instructions

Directions:

1. Mix the garlic, onion, chicken powder, paprika, salt and pepper in a mixing bowl. Add the chicken and toss it with your hands to coat it completely with the spices.
2. Select the 'Sauté' mode and preheat the Instant Pot. When the pot gets hot, add the butter and oil and stir until the butter is completely melted. Add the chicken a few pieces at a time and sauté them on both sides.
3. When all the chicken has been sautéed, add the chicken broth to the pot. Secure the lid and cook on high pressure for 3 minutes using the 'Manual' mode. When the time is up, do a quick release of the pressure.

4. In a small bowl, dissolve cornstarch in water. Add it to the pot, and stir to combine. Mix well.
5. Select the 'Sauté' mode again and stir until the sauce thickens. Take the sauce and chicken out and stir in heavy cream. Serve with spaghetti sprinkled with parsley. Enjoy!

Recipe # 25: Cola Chicken Wings:

Serves: 2 to 4 people

Prep Time: 5 minutes

Cooking Time: 25 minutes

Ingredients:

1. 1 1/2 pounds' of chicken wings
2. 1 stalk green onion, 2 inch pieces
3. 4 cloves of garlic, crushed finely
4. 1 tablespoon of ginger
5. 200 mL Coca Cola
6. 1 tablespoon of dark soy sauce
7. 2 tablespoons of light soy sauce
8. 1 tablespoon of peanut oil
9. 1 tablespoon of Chinese rice wine

Directions:

1. Preheat the Instant Pot and set the mode to 'Sauté'. Add the peanut oil, garlic, ginger and green onions into the pot, then let it cook for a minute. Add the chicken wings and stir for roughly one to two minutes.
2. When the edges of the chicken start getting brown, add the sauces, wine and mix properly. Thereafter cover the lid and cook on a high pressure for 5 minutes using the 'Manual' mode.
3. When the time is up, let the pressure naturally release itself. Taste the wings,

sauce, then add more seasoning sauce and salt if required. Serve immediately with rice or other dishes. Enjoy!

Recipe # 26: Cranberry Braised Turkey Wings:

Serves: 6 to 8 people

Prep Time: 10 minutes

Cooking Time: 25 minutes

Ingredients:

1. 2 tablespoons of oil
2. 2 tablespoons of butter
3. 4 turkey wings, 2 to 3 pounds
4. salt, according to taste
5. pepper, according to taste
6. 1 cup of dried cranberries, soaked in water
7. 1 onion, sliced
8. 1 cup of orange juice
9. 1 cup of walnuts
10. 1 cup of vegetable stock
11. 1 bunch thyme

Directions:

1. Preheat the Instant Pot using the 'Sauté' function, then melt the butter and add the olive oil. Place the turkey wings in the Instant Pot and make it brownish on both sides, adding the salt and pepper to taste.
2. Remove the wings when browned and add the onions, followed by the wings again with the brown side facing upwards. Then add the cranberries, walnuts,thyme and pour the orange juice/stock in the pot as well.
3. Cover the lid, and then cook for 20 minutes on a high pressure using the

'Manual' mode. When the time is up, remove the thyme and move the wings to a serving dish.

4. Place the wings to a broiler for 5 minutes, and when the wings caramelize, reduce the remaining contents by half using the 'Sauté' mode.
5. Pour the liquid over the wings and Enjoy!

Recipe # 27: Easy BBQ Chicken Thighs:

Serves: 4 people

Prep Time: 5 minutes

Cooking Time: 30 minutes

Ingredients:

1. 1 teaspoon of olive oil
2. 1 medium sized onion, sliced
3. 2 pounds' of chicken, skinless
4. 1 cup of barbeque sauce
5. 1/4 cup of honey
6. 1/2 cup of ketchup
7. 1/2 teaspoon of black pepper
8. 1 teaspoon of salt
9. 1/4 teaspoon of cumin
10. 1/4 teaspoon of onion powder
11. 1/4 teaspoon of garlic powder
12. ¼ teaspoon of smoked paprika
13. 1/4 teaspoon of paprika
14. pinch chili flakes

Directions:

1. Preheat the Instant Pot using the 'Sauté' option and add the oil. When it is

heated, add the chicken and brown each side for 3 minutes. While the chicken is browning, mix the remaining ingredients in a mixing bowl.

2. Spread the onion around the chicken and cover it with the sauce. Cook on a high pressure for 10 minutes using the 'Manual' mode.

3. While the chicken is cooking, line a sheet pan with the foil and set the broiler to a high pressure. When the chicken is done, remove the chicken with thetongs (as it will be falling apart) and place it under the broiler for 3 minutes on each side.

4. While the chicken is browning, switch to the 'Sauté' mode and cook until the sauce has reduced to about half the volume. Once done, pour it over on the browned chicken. Enjoy!

Recipe # 28: Indian Style Apricot Chicken:

Serves: 4 people

Prep Time: 20 minutes

Cooking Time: 11 minutes

Ingredients:

1. 2 1/2 pounds' of chicken thighs, skinless
2. 1/2 teaspoon of salt
3. 1/4 teaspoon of black pepper
4. 1 teaspoon of vegetable oil
5. 1 large onion, chopped
6. 1/2 cup of chicken broth
7. 1 tablespoon of ginger, freshly grated
8. 2 cloves of garlic, minced
9. 1/2 teaspoon of ground cinnamon
10. 1/8 teaspoon of ground allspice
11. 1 can diced tomatoes

12. 1 package of dried apricots
13. 1 pinch of saffron threads, optional
14. Italian parsley, optional

Directions:

1. Season the chicken with salt and pepper, then cook the chicken in batches using the 'Sauté' mode of the Instant Pot for 8 minutes on each batch. Remove the chicken and place it in a plate.
2. Add the onion and 2 tablespoons of chicken broth to the pot, then cook for 5 minutes until the onion is translucent, while making sure to scrap the burnt ones from the bottom of the pot.
3. Add the ginger, garlic, cinnamon, allspice and cook for 30 seconds until it starts producing fragrance. Pour in the tomatoes, apricots, the remaining broth, saffron, and mix properly. Return the chicken to the Instant Pot, and cook on high pressure for 11 minutes using the 'Manual' setting.
4. Once done, use a quick release to get rid of the pressure, season it with salt and pepper, then garnish it with parsley if desired. Enjoy!

Recipe # 29: Honey Garlic Chicken Lettuce Wraps:

Serves: 4 to 6 people

Prep Time: 30 minutes

Cooking Time: 30 minutes

Ingredients:

1. 2 tablespoons of coconut aminos
2. 1/8 cup of honey garlic sauce
3. 1/4 teaspoon of chilies
4. 1 tablespoon of onion, minced
5. 1/2 teaspoon of salt

6. 1 teaspoon of black pepper
7. 8 to 10 chicken thighs, bone and skinless
8. 1 jalapeno, sliced(optional)
9. 1 head lettuce
10. 1 medium carrot, finely grated
11. 1/2 bell of pepper, thinly sliced
12. 1 green onion, diced
13. 1 avocado, thinly sliced
14. 1/8 cup of cashews, chopped

Directions:

1. Combine the coconut aminos, onions, chilies, salt, pepper and the honey garlic sauce in a bowl. Add the chicken to the mixture and let it soak for 20 to 40 minutes.
2. Put the chicken , the sauce, in the Instant Pot, and cook on a high pressure for 6 minutes using the 'Manual' mode. While waiting for that, you can chop, grate the ingredients listed above and prepare the lettuce into full leaves.
3. Once the time is exhausted, let the pressure manually release. Thereafter, leave it in the sauce until you are ready to wrap it up. Then place the chicken, carrot, pepper, cashews, onions and avocado in the leaves of the lettuce, and roll it up. Serve and enjoy!

Recipe # 30: Teriyaki Chicken and Rice:

Serves: 4 to 6 people

Prep Time: 25 minutes

Cooking Time: 30 minutes

Ingredients:

1. 6 chicken thighs, bone-in with skin

2. 1 slice of ginger, very thin
3. 4 crushed garlic cloves
4. 1 1/2 tablespoons of cornstarch, mixed with
   2 tablespoons of water
5. teriyaki sauce
6. 4 tablespoons of Japanese Cooking Rice Wine
7. 4 tablespoons of Japanese soy sauce
8. 4 tablespoons of Japanese cooking sake
9. 1/4 teaspoon of sesame oil
10. 2 tablespoons of white sugar
11. 1 1/2 cup of water
12. 1 cup of calrose rice, medium grain

Directions:

1. Mix the soy sauce, sake, mirin, sugar and sesame oil to create the teriyaki sauce mixture. Then soak the chicken with the sauce for 20 minutes.
2. Pour the marinade (without the chicken) into the Instant Pot and cook using the 'Sauté' mode. Add the garlic cloves, ginger, to the mixture and let it boil for 30 seconds or until the alcohol evaporates.
3. Add the chicken to the Instant Pot, pour the rice into a steamer rack, insert it into the pressure cooker and pour the water into the bowl of rice, making sure all of it is soaked in the water.
4. Cover the lid and cook on a high pressure for 6 minutes. When the time is up, use the quick pressure release to remove the pressure.
5. Set the rice, chicken, ginger and garlic aside, and heat the remaining seasoning using the 'Sauté' mode. Add the cornstarch into the sauce slowly until you reach your desired thickness. Then serve immediately with rice and other side dishes. Enjoy!

Recipe # 31: Salt Baked Chicken:

Serves: 8 people

Prep Time: 5 minutes

Cooking Time: 45 minutes

Ingredients:

1. 2 teaspoons of sand ginger, dried
2. 1 1/4 teaspoon of kosher salt
3. 1/4 teaspoon of 5 spice powder
4. 8 chicken drumsticks

Directions:

1. Season the chicken legs by covering it with a mixture of kosher salt, 5 spice powder and a sand ginger. Mix properly and place the seasoned legs on a large piece of parchment paper (Do not use aluminum foil).
2. Place the steamer rack above the Instant Pot and pour one cup of water on it. Place the legs dish into the rack and cover the lid of the pot. Cook on a high pressure for 20 minutes, and then let the pressure release naturally.
3. Remove the dish from the Instant Pot and carefully unwrap the parchment paper. Serve immediately. Enjoy!

Recipe # 32: Chinese Simmered Chicken:

Serves: 6 people

Prep Time: 6 minutes

Cooking Time: 15 minutes

Ingredients:

1. 1/3 cup of soy sauce
2. 1/3 cup of brown sugar

3. 1/4 cup of water
4. 1/4 cup of dry sherry or apple juice
5. 1 tablespoon of ketchup
6. 1/2 teaspoon of red pepper flakes, crushed
7. 1 clove garlic, minced
8. 1 scallion sliced
9. 2 tablespoons of cornstarch
10. 2 teaspoons of sesame seeds
11. rice, cooked
12. 4 pounds' of chicken, boneless and skinless
13. 1 tablespoon of olive oil

Directions:

1. Combine the soy sauce, sugar, water, sherry, ketchup, red pepper flakes, garlic, and scallion into a mixing bowl and whisk properly. This will be your sauce.
2. Select the 'Sauté' mode on the Instant Pot and pour the oil into the pot. Lightly sear the chicken in the pot and deglaze the Instant Pot with the sherry and add the sauce, while mixing properly.
3. Add the rice, and cover the lid. Cook at a high pressure for 6 minutes, and when the time is up, use a natural pressure release, and select the 'Sauté' mode again.
4. Remove the rice, chicken, the half cup of the sauce into a platter and add the potato starch into the remaining sauce in the Instant Pot. Cook until the sauce is thick and sticky.
5. Pour the thickened sauce over the chicken, serve with rice and theremaining sauce. Thereafter, garnish it with sesame seeds. Enjoy!

Recipe # 33: Buffalo Hot Wings:

Serves: 6 people

Prep Time: 5 minutes

Cooking Time: 15 minutes

Ingredients:

1. 4 pounds' chicken wings
2. 1/2 cup of butter
3. 1/2 cup of Frank's Red Hot Cayenne Pepper Sauce
4. 1 tablespoon of Worcestershire sauce
5. 1/2 teaspoon of kosher salt
6. 3/4 cup of water
7. 1 to 2 tablespoon of light brown sugar

Directions:

1. Mix the pepper sauce, butter, Worcestershire, brown sugar , salt, and microwave all of it for 15 seconds, or until the butter is melted.
2. Pour the water into the Instant Pot, and place the wings on a trivet. Cook at a high pressure for 5 minutes with the lid covered. When done, let the pressure release itself naturally.
3. Place an oven rack in the center of the oven and turn it on to Broil. Brush the chicken wings gently and place them on the oven rack on a cookie sheet. Broil for 5 minutes on each side, or repeat until it gets crispy.
4. Remove the chicken and serve immediately with the remaining sauce. Enjoy!

Recipe # 34: Ligurian Lemon Chicken:

Serves: 6 people

Prep Time: 10 minutes

Cooking Time: 15 minutes

Ingredients:

1. 1 chicken, cut into 8 pieces

2. 1 cup of vegetable or chicken stock
3. 4 ounces' of black olives
4. 1/2 cup of dry white wine
5. 4 lemons, 3 juiced and one for garnish
6. 2 cloves of garlic
7. 3 sprigs of rosemary, one for garnish, and two for chopping
8. 2 sprigs sage
9. 1/2 bunch of Parsley leaves
10. salt and pepper, to taste
11. 4 tablespoons of olive oil

Directions:

1. Prepare the marinade by finely chopping the garlic, sage, parsley and the rosemary. Place them into a container and add the lemon juice, oil, salt, pepper. and mix properly.
2. Place the chicken in a dish and cover it properly with the marinade, a plastic wrap and leave it in the fridge for 4 hours. Using the 'Sauté' mode, cook the chicken for 5 minutes on each sid and when its done , set it aside.
3. Deglaze the Instant Pot with the wine until it evaporates. Add the chicken back in, pour the leftover marinade and place it on top of everything. Thereafter, cover the lid and cook on a high pressure for 12 minutes using the 'Manual' setting.
4. Take the chicken out and reduce the liquid in the pot to about 1/4 of its original amount. Pour the sauce over the chicken, serve with a sprinkle of rosemary, olives and the fresh lemon slices. Enjoy!

Recipe # 35: Not Yo Mama's Chicken Korma:

Serves: 6 people

Prep Time: 5 minutes

<u>Cooking Time:</u> 20 minutes

<u>Ingredients:</u>

1. 1-pound of chicken, breasts or legs, boneless
2. 1 ounce of cashews, raw
3. 1 small onion, chopped
4. 1/2 cup of tomatoes, diced
5. 1/2 green of Serrano pepper, Thai Chile pepper
6. 5 cloves of garlic
7. 1 teaspoon of Ginger, minced
8. 1 teaspoon of turmeric
9. 1 teaspoon of salt
10. 1 teaspoon of garam masala
11. 1 teaspoon of cumin-coriander powder
12. 1/2 teaspoon of cayenne pepper
13. 1/2 cup of water, for sloshing the blender and for preheating the Instant Pot
14. 1 teaspoon of garam masala, for finishing
15. 1/2 cup of coconut milk, full fat
16. 1/4 cup of cilantro

<u>Directions:</u>

1. Blend all the ingredients except for the chicken, garam masala, coconut milk and cilantro. Pour the sauce in the Instant Pot, top it with the chicken and cook on a high pressure for 10 minutes.
2. When the time is up, let the pressure release naturally. After that, take the chicken out and cut it into small pieces. Then add the coconut milk and garam masala, garnish it with the cilantro and serve. Enjoy!

Recipe # 36: Salsa Chicken:

Serves: 4 to 5 people

Prep Time: 5 minutes

Cooking Time: 25 minutes

Ingredients:

1. 2 chicken breasts, boneless and skinless
2. sea salt
3. Mexican seasoning (chili, taco or fajita)
4. 1 cup of salsa, your preference

Direction:

1. Season the chicken with salt and other seasonings on both sides. Place the breasts directly in the Instant Pot, and top it with the salsa. Cook for 10 minutes on a high pressure using the 'Manual' mode.
2. Then when time is exhausted, let the pressure release naturally for 10 minutes. Use the tongs to transfer the chicken and the forks to shred the chicken into small pieces.
3. Serve it with the casseroles, or simply add to the corn tortillas, some avocado, cilantro and lime juice for a quick meal. Enjoy!

Recipe # 37: Turkey and White Bean Chili:

Serves: 4 people

Prep Time: 10 minutes

Cooking Time: 50 minutes

Ingredients:

1. 1 tablespoon of olive oil
2. 1/2 cup of Anahiem pepper, diced
3. 2 cups of yellow onion, diced
4. 1-pound of ground turkey
5. 1/2 cup of red bell pepper, diced
6. 1 tablespoon of salt
7. 1/2 teaspoon of black pepper
8. 1 teaspoon of oregano
9. 2 tablespoons of chili powder
10. 1 cup of cannellini beans, pre-soaked for 12 hours
11. 2 1/2 cups of chicken stock
12. sour cream, for serving
13. cilantro, chopped for serving
14. Spicy Monterey Jack cheese, for serving

Directions:

1. Set Instant Pot to the 'Sauté' mode and add the oil, onion and peppers. Cook it the onions become brownish.. Then add the turkey, seasonings, and heat it until it gets almost cooked, about 10 minutes.
2. Add the beans, water and the chicken stock. Cover the lid and cook it for 30 minutes using the 'Bean/Chili' mode. When the time is up, release the pressure and serve it with the sour cream, cilantro and Spicy Monterey Jack cheese. Enjoy!

Recipe # 38: Mergherita Chicken with Sundried Tomato Sauce:

Serves: 4 people

Prep Time: 10 minutes

Cooking Time: 25 minutes

Ingredients:

1. 1/4 cup of balsamic vinegar
2. 1 tablespoon of olive oil
3. 2 tablespoons of Dijon mustard
4. 2 tablespoons of lemon juice
5. 2 cloves of garlic, minced
6. 1/2 teaspoon of Himalayan salt
7. 1/4 teaspoon of pepper
8. 6 chicken breasts, boneless and skinless
9. 2 teaspoons of butter
10. 1 cup of chicken bone broth
11. 1/2 cup of sundried tomatoes
12. 1 tablespoon of parsley
13. 1 teaspoon of lemon zest

Directions:

1. Whisk the mustard, vinegar, lemon juice, olive oil, pepper and the garlic salt in small bowl. Mix the vinaigrette, chicken pieces, in a plastic bag and cover by tossing it.
2. Refrigerate it for at least 2 hours to one day. Set the Instant Pot to the 'sauté' mode, melt the butter and get the chicken breasts brown.
3. Remove the chicken from the cooker and deglaze the Pot with chicken bone broth. Add the sundried tomatoes, parsley, lemon zest and return the chicken to the Instant Pot.
4. Cook on a high pressure for 8 minutes on the 'Manual' mode, and when the time is up, allow the pressure to release. Serve and Enjoy!

Recipe # 39: Lemon and Herb Chicken:

Serves: 6 people

Prep Time: 20 minutes

Cooking Time: 25 minutes

Ingredients:

1. 4 pounds of white chicken
2. 1 tablespoon of olive oil
3. 1 tablespoon of butter, melted
4. 1/2 teaspoon of black pepper
5. 1 teaspoon of Pink Himalayan salt
6. 1 cup of chicken bone broth
7. 1/2 yellow onion, quartered
8. 1/2 lemon, sliced
9. several sprig of herbs
10. 1 cup of chicken bone broth

Directions:

1. Rub the chicken breast with the olive oil, butter and season it with the salt and pepper. Preheat the Instant Pot using the 'Sauté' mode, and place the chicken in the Pot.
2. Brown the chicken for at least 2 minutes or until the chicken turns a fully golden brown color. Remove the chicken to a place and deglaze the pan with the bone broth.
3. Put the lemons, garlic, onion and fresh herbs into the cavity of the whole chicken and return it to the Instant Pot. Using the 'Manual' mode, cook the chicken for 20 minutes on a high pressure.
4. Transfer the chicken to the plate, and serve with the broth. Enjoy!

Recipe # 40: Honey Garlic Chicken Wings:

Serves: 4 people

Prep Time: 10 minutes

Cooking Time: 10 minutes

Ingredients:

1. 1 1/2 pounds' of chicken wings
2. 1/2 shallot, roughly minced
3. 1 to 2-star anise
4. 1 tablespoon of ginger, sliced
5. 4 cloves of garlic, roughly minced
6. 1 tablespoon of honey
7. 1/2 cup of water, warm
8. 1 1/2 tablespoon of cornstarch
9. 1 tablespoon of peanut oil
10. 2 tablespoon of light soy sauce
11. 1 tablespoon of dark soy sauce
12. 1 teaspoon of sugar
13. 1 tablespoon of Shaoxing wine
14. 1/4 teaspoon of salt

Directions:

1. Make the marinade by mixing the light and dark soy sauce, Shaoxing wine, sugar and the salt. Soak the chicken wings for 20 minutes.
2. Heat up the Instant Pot using the 'Sauté' mode and add the peanut oil to the base. Add the chicken wings, then brown the chicken wings for 30 seconds on each side. Then remove and set it aside.
3. Add the shallot, star anise, sliced ginger and then stir for a minute. Add the garlic and continue stirring until it produces some fragrance. Mix the honey with a warm water and add it to the bottom of the pot. Place the chicken wings into the pot, cover the lid and cook it on a high pressure for 5 minutes using the 'Manual' mode.
4. Once the time is up, remove the chicken wings only. Using the sauté mode, add the cornstarch with one tablespoon of cold water and then keep mixing until it gets to your desired thickness.
5. Add the chicken wings back into the Instant Pot and then transfer all of it to a large bowl. Serve immediately. Enjoy!

Vegetarian:

Recipe # 41: Cauliflower Potato Curry:

Serves: 4 people

Prep Time: 10 minutes

Cooking Time: 10 minutes

Ingredients:

1. 1 medium sized onion, thinly sliced
2. 2 plum tomatoes, diced
3. 1 medium potato, cut into wedges
4. 4 cups of cauliflower, big 2 inch pieces
5. 1 tablespoon of cooking oil
6. 1/2 teaspoon of cumin
7. 1/2 teaspoon of turmeric
8. 1 teaspoon of mild red chili powder
9. 1 tablespoon of cumin-coriander
10. 1 teaspoon of salt
11. 1 1/2 teaspoon of garam masala

Directions:

1. Preheat the Instant Pot using the 'Sauté' mode. Add the oil, cumin and sauté it for 30 seconds. Add the onions and cook it for an additional 1 minute. Add the tomatoes and cook for 1 more minute too.
2. Add the turmeric, red chili powder, cumin-coriander, garam masala, the salt and keep mixing properly. Add the potatoes, cauliflower and 1/4 cup of water as well.
3. Cover the lid and cook for 3 minutes on high pressure using the 'Manual' mode. Increase the time by 2 minutes if you want a firmer cauliflower.
4. When the time is up, quick release the pressure and take the curry out of the Instant Pot. Serve it with a toasted pita bread. Enjoy!

Recipe # 42: BBQ Cabbage Sandwiches:

Serves: 6 people

Prep Time: 5 minutes

Cooking Time: 10 minutes

Ingredients:

1. 1 head cabbage, chopped
2. 1 yellow onion, small and thinly sliced
3. 2 1/2 cups of BBQ sauce
4. 6 buns, whole wheat and gluten free

Directions:

1. Preheat the Instant Pot using the 'Sauté' mode, and add 2 tablespoons of water to the pot. Add cabbage, onion, and heat it until they are softened, usually at about 4 minutes. Thereafter, add the BBQ sauce and cook for 3 more minutes.
2. Stop the 'Sauté' mode, toast the buns, fill them with thee BBQ cabbage and serve immediately. Enjoy!

Recipe # 43: BBQ Lentils over Baked Potato Wedges:

Serves: 4 people

Prep Time: 5 minutes

Cooking Time: 20 minutes

Ingredients:

1. 3 cup of water
2. 1 small onion, chopped

3. 1/2 cup of ketchup, organic
4. 1 cup of brown lentils, dry and drained
5. 2 teaspoons of liquid smoke
6. 2 teaspoons of molasses
7. 2 large potatoes, baked and cut into 6 wedges

Directions:

1. Place the lentils, water, the onion in the Instant Pot and cook for 10 minutes on a high pressure using the 'Manual' mode. When the time is up, let the pressure naturally release.
2. Add the ketchup, molasses, liquid smoke to the pot and then using the 'Sauté' mode, simmer it for 5 minutes. When the time is up, stop the 'Sauté' mode and serve it over some baked potato wedges. Enjoy!

Recipe # 44: Bell Peppers and Stir Fried Potatoes:

Serves: 2 people

Prep Time: 5 minutes

Cooking Time: 15 minutes

Ingredients:

1. 1 tablespoon of oil
2. 2 bell pepper, cut into long pieces
3. 1/2 teaspoon of cumin seeds
4. 4 baby potatoes, cut into small pieces
5. 1/2 teaspoon of dry mango
6. 1/4 teaspoon of turmeric
7. 1/2 teaspoon of cayenne
8. 2 teaspoon of coriander
9. 1 teaspoon of salt

10. 4 cloves of garlic
11. cilantro, for garnishing

Directions:

1. Preheat the Instant Pot using the 'Sauté' mode, add the oil, cumin and garlic. Once the garlic turns golden brown, add the peppers, spices and potatoes. Thereafter, sprinkle the water and mix properly.
2. Change the mode to 'Manual' and cook on a high pressure for 2 minutes. When done, release the pressure manually. If the mixture is watery, simmer it using the 'Sauté' mode with the lid open and stir until you get the desired consistency.
3. Add the dry mango or lemon juice and mix evenly. Garnish it with the cilantro and serve with a yogurt. Enjoy!

Recipe # 45: Black Bean Mushroom Chili:

Serves: 4 to 6 people

Prep Time: 5 minutes

Cooking Time: 16 minutes

Ingredients:

1. 3 cups of onion, chopped
2. 8 cloves of garlic, finely minced
3. 2 pounds' of mushrooms, sliced
4. 2 cans of fire roasted tomatoes
5. 16 ounces' of corn, frozen
6. 3 cans of black beans, including liquid
7. 1 tablespoon of grounded cumin
8. 1 oregano
9. 1/2 tablespoon of smoked paprika

10. 1/2 teaspoon of ground chipotle powder
11. 1 cup of oats
12. 1 cup of nutritional yeast
13. 1 tablespoon of salt-free seasoning

Directions:

1. Preheat the Instant Pot using the 'Sauté' mode, then heat the onions until they are brown at about 10 minutes, while constantly adding small amounts of water to prevent sticking. Then add the garlic and heat it for one more minute.
2. Change the mode to 'Manual' and add all the ingredients except for the corn and the Faux Parmesan. Cook on a high pressure for 6 minutes, and let the pressure naturally release.
3. While the dish is cooking, place the faux ingredients into a food processor and grind until it turns into powder. This powder is usually known as the Faux Parmesan.
4. When the pressure is released, pour the curry into a bowl. Stir in the corn and sprinkle the Faux Parmesan on topof it. Enjoy!

Recipe # 46: Chickpea Curry:

Serves: 4 to 6 people

Prep Time: 10 minutes

Cooking Time: 5 minutes

Ingredients:

1. 1 onion, diced
2. 2 cloves of garlic, minced
3. 2 tablespoons of extra-virgin olive oil
4. 1 small green bell pepper, diced
5. 2 cans of chickpeas, rinsed and drained

6. 1 can of tomatoes, crushed or diced, with juice
7. 1 tablespoon of curry powder
8. 1 cup of corn, frozen
9. 1 packed cup of kale, chopped
10. 1 cup of okra, frozen and sliced
11. 1 cup of vegetable broth
12. 1 tablespoon of honey or sugar
13. 1 teaspoon of kosher salt
14. 1/4 teaspoon of black pepper, freshly grounded
15. 2 tablespoon of cilantro leaves, for garnishing
16. 1 lime, juiced.

Directions:

1. Preheat the Instant Pot using the 'Sauté' mode, add the oil and onion. Cook for 4 minutes, then add the bell pepper, garlic and cook for 2 more minutes.
2. Add the curry powder and stir it for 30 seconds. Add the chickpeas, tomatoes, corn, okra, kale, broth, and honey (or sugar). Cover the lid and cook for 5 minutes on a high pressure using the 'Manual' mode. Once the cooking is done, let the pressure naturally release.
3. Add the salt, pepper, and lime juice. Stir it until it mixes properly, while adding more salt as desired. Top it with the cilantro leaves and serve. Enjoy!

Recipe # 47: Couscous and Vegetable Medley:

Serves: 3 people

Prep Time: 5 minutes

Cooking Time: 20 minutes

Ingredients:

1. 1 tablespoon of olive oil

2. 2 bay leaves, or Taj Patta
3. 1 large red bell pepper, chopped
4. 1/2 large onion, chopped
5. 1 3/4 cup of couscous Israeli
6. 1 cup of carrot, grated
7. 1 3/4 cup of water
8. 2 teaspoon of salt, according to taste
9. 1/2 teaspoon of garam masala
10. 1 tablespoon of lemon juice
11. cilantro, for garnishing

Directions:

1. Preheat the Instant Pot to the 'sauté' mode and add the olive oil, bay leaves and onions. Heat it for 2 minutes, add the bell peppers, carrots and sauté it for one more minute. Add the couscous, water, salt, garam masala and mix properly.
2. Change the mode to 'Manual' and cook for 2 minutes. When the time is up, do a 10-minute natural pressure release and fluff the couscous until it is fully cooked. Mix the lemon juice, garnish it with the cilantro and serve it hot. Enjoy!

Recipe # 48: Kashmiri Potato Curry:

Serves: 3 people

Prep Time: 10 minutes

Cooking Time: 20 minutes

Ingredients:

1. 10 baby potatoes, peeled and cored.
2. 1 onion, finely chopped

3. 2 tablespoons of ghee
4. 2 teaspoons of ginger, grated
5. 2 red tomatoes, pureed
6. 2 teaspoon of garlic, grated
7. 1/2 teaspoon of turmeric
8. 1 teaspoon of Kashmiri red chili powder
9. 1 teaspoon of salt
10. 8 to 10 cashews
11. 1/4 cup of warm milk
12. 1 tablespoon of dried fenugreek leaves
13. some cilantro leaves

Directions:

1. Preheat the Instant Pot using the 'Sauté' mode. Add the ghee, onions and cook for 2 minutes while constantly stirring, then add the ginger, potatoes and garlic paste for 30 seconds.
2. Add the tomato paste, red chili powder, turmeric, garam masala and salt. Cook everything for two minutes while constantly stirring. With a small spoon, carefully fill the potatoes and line them all in the space of the Instant Pot.
3. Add 1.2 cup of water, cover the lid, then cook for 8 minutes on a high pressure using the 'Manual' mode. When the time is up, quickly release the pressure.
4. Blend the milk and cashews to make a smooth paste, then add the liquid, dried fenugreek leaves, cashew paste and the cilantro leaves. Set the nstant Pot to the 'Sauté' mode and mix together. Add the salt, then turn the Instant Pot off.
5. Serve with rice. Enjoy!

Recipe # 49: Easy Potato Beans:

Serves: 3 people

Prep Time: 5 minutes

Cooking Time: 10 minutes

Ingredients:

1. 1 tablespoon of oil
2. 4 cloves of garlic, chopped
3. 1/2 teaspoon of cumin seeds
4. 1 green chili, chopped
5. 2 cup of green beans, 1/2 inch pieces
6. 1 potato, cubed into small pieces
7. 2 teaspoons of coriander powder
8. 1/4 teaspoon of turmeric
9. 1/4 teaspoon of red chili
10. 1 1/2 teaspoons of salt
11. 1 teaspoon of dry mango,

Directions:

1. Preheat the Instant Pot using the 'Sauté' mode. Add the oil, cumin seeds, green chili and garlic. When the seeds start to splutter, add the green beans and potatoes. Combine all the spices except the dry mango, and mix properly. Thereafter, sprinkle some water on top of it.
2. Secure the Instant Pot, and cook for 2 minutes on a high pressure using the 'Manual' mode. When the time is up, let the pressure naturally release itself. Mix the dry mango into the curry,serve with a bread and enjoy!

Recipe # 50: Green Coconut Curry:

Serves: 4 people

Prep Time: 5 minutes

Cooking Time: 15 minutes

Ingredients:

1. 1/2 cup of chickpeas, soaked for 6 hours
2. 1 small onion, diced
3. 2 cloves of garlic, minced
4. 1 teaspoon of turmeric, freshly minced
5. 2 teaspoons of ginger, freshly minced
6. 1 can of coconut milk
7. 1/2 cup of vegetable stock
8. 1 tablespoon of green curry paste
9. 1/2 teaspoon of cumin
10. 1/2 teaspoon of black pepper
11. 1 teaspoon of salt
12. 1/2 teaspoon of curry
13. 1/4 teaspoon of ground coriander
14. 1/4 teaspoon of chili powder
15. 1 cup of spinach
16. 2 teaspoon of lemon juice

Directions:

1. Preheat the Instant Pot using the 'Sauté' mode and add the onions. Heat it until they are brownish, then add the ginger, garlic and turmeric. Sauté it for 2 more minutes and add all the remaining ingredients except for the lemon juice and spinach.
2. Cover the lid and change the mode to 'Manual'. Cook on a high pressure for 15 minutes and when the time has elapsed, allow a natural pressure release.
3. Add the spinach and lemon juice on top and stir well. Serve and Enjoy!

Recipe # 51: Instant Potatouille:

Serves: 4 people

Prep Time: 5 minutes

Cooking Time: 10 minutes

Ingredients:

1. 1/4 cup of water
2. 4 ounces of Yellow Crookneck Squash
3. 4 ounces of Zucchini
4. 6 ounces of Chinese Eggplant
5. 4 ounces of Orange Bell Pepper
6. 3 ounces of Portobello mushrooms
7. 1/4 red onion
8. 12 ounces of Yukon gold potatoes, about 1 1/2 pounds
9. 1 can of Fire Roasted Tomatoes
10. 1/4 cup of basil, finely chopped into threads

Directions:

1. Put all the ingredients except the basil into into the Instant Pot and cook on a high pressure for 10 minutes using the 'Manual' mode. Once done, quick release the pressure and pour in the basil.
2. Serve it with rice if desired. Enjoy!

Recipe # 52: Italian Cannellini and Mint Salad:

Serves: 4 people

Prep Time: 1 minute

Cooking Time: 8 minutes

Ingredients:

1. 1 cup of cannellini beans, soaked in water
2. 4 cups of warm water
3. 1 clove of garlic, smashed

4. 1 bay leaf
5. 1 sprig mint, fresh
6. 1 dash of vinegar
7. olive oil
8. salt and pepper, to taste

Directions:

1. Place the beans, water, garlic and bay leaf into the Instant Pot, cover the lid and cook on a high pressure for 8 minutes using the 'Manual' mode. When the time has elapsed, use a natural pressure release.
2. Mix the mint, vinegar, oil, salt, pepper and stir well. Serve and Enjoy!

Recipe # 53: Lemon-Sage Spaghetti Squash:

Serves: 4 people

Prep Time: 15 minutes

Cooking Time: 9 minutes

Ingredients:

1. 2 pounds' of spaghetti squash, cut into half
2. 1 cup of water
3. 2 tablespoons of butter
4. 1/4 cup of onion, chopped
5. 2 garlic cloves, minced
6. 2 tablespoons of Parmesan cheese, grated
7. 2 tablespoons of sage leaves, finely chopped
8. 1 teaspoon of lemon rind, grated
9. 1/2 teaspoon of table salt
10. 1/4 teaspoon of black pepper, grounded

Directions:

1. Place a steam rack in the inner pot of the Instant Pot, and pour the water. Add the squash halves, and cook at a high pressure for 9 minutes using the 'Manual' mode. When done, lift the squash using rack handles and set it aside to cool down.
2. While the squash is cooling, pour the water the from the inner pot,rinse it well,dry it and return it to the cooker. When the squash cools down, use a fork to remove the spaghetti-like strands in a bowl.
3. Add the butter into the Instant Pot, and heat it using the 'Sauté' mode. When the butter melts, add the onion,garlic and cook for 2 minutes while constantly stirring. Then, add the squash to the pot, stir for 2 more minutes and transfer again to the bowl.
4. Add the Parmesan cheese and other ingredients on top and serve. Enjoy!

Recipe # 54: Lentil and Red Bean Chili:

Serves: 6 people

Prep Time: 15 minutes

Cooking Time: 45 minutes

Ingredients:

1. 1/2 cup of brown and red lentils, soaked in water overnight
2. 1/2 cup of yellow onion, chopped
3. 1 cup of carrot, chopped
4. 1 green bell pepper, chopped
5. 5 cloves of garlic, minced
6. 1 teaspoon of smoked paprika
7. 1 1/2 teaspoons of chili powder
8. 1/2 teaspoon of coriander powder
9. 1 teaspoon of cumin powder
10. 1/2 teaspoon of dried oregano

11. 1/2 teaspoon of allspice
12. 1/2 teaspoon of cayenne powder
13. 1 teaspoon of salt
14. 2 tablespoons of coconut aminos
15. 1 can of tomatoes, diced
16. 1/4 heaping cup of tomato paste
17. 1 1/2 cups of water
18. 1 cup of corn

Directions:

1. Preheat the Instant Pot using the 'Sauté' mode, add the carrots, onions, garlic, bell pepper and sauté for 3 to 5 minutes, stirring occasionally.
2. Add all the spices, salt, coconut aminos, tomatoes, tomato paste and beans. Stir for one minute then add the water and stir once more.
3. Cover the lid of the Instant Pot and cook for 30 minutes on a high pressure using the 'Manual' mode. Once done, let the pressure naturally release. Then after opening the lid, add the corn and stir properly.
4. Allow the chili to cool off before you serve or store in the fridge. Enjoy!

Recipe # 55: Lentils and Farro:

Serves: 2 people

Prep Time: 2 minutes

Cooking Time: 12 minutes

Ingredients:

1. 1/2 cup of lentils, brown, black or green
2. 1 1/4 cup of water
3. 1/2 teaspoon of medium chili powder
4. 1/2 teaspoon of dried oregano

5. 1/2 teaspoon of salt
6. 1/2 teaspoon of dried basil
7. 1/4 teaspoon of cumin powder
8. 1/4 teaspoon of smoked paprika
9. 1/4 teaspoon of onion powder
10. 1/4 teaspoon of garlic powder
11. 1/4 teaspoon of black pepper
12. 1/2 cup of Farro, for Farro
13. 1 cup of water, for Farro
14. 1/2 teaspoon of Italian herbs, for Farro
15. 1/2 teaspoon of onion powder, for Farro
16. 1/2 teaspoon of salt, for Farro

Directions:

1. Add all the ingredients except the Farro ones into the Instant Pot. Place the trivet on top of lentils, add the faro ingredients in it and cover the lid. Cook for 12 minutes on a high pressure using the 'Manual' mode.
2. When the time has elapsed, let the pressure naturally release. Serve it with your favorite veggies and sauces. Enjoy!

Recipe # 56: Middle Eastern Millet Pilaf:

Serves: 4 people

Prep Time: 5 minutes

Cooking Time: 10 minutes

Ingredients:

1. 1 tablespoon of oil
2. 1 cup of onion, chopped
3. 2 cloves of garlic, minced

4. 1 stick of cinnamon
5. 1 cup of carrots, roughly chopped
6. 1 cup of millet
7. 1 3/4 cups of water
8. salt, to taste
9. pepper, to taste
10. Italian parsley, chopped

Directions:

1. Heat the oil in the Instant Pot using the 'Sauté' mode. Add the onions and heat it for one minute. Add the garlic, carrots, cinnamon stick and heat it for 30 more seconds. Thereafter, add the millet, water and stir.
2. Cover the lid of the Instant Pot and cook for 10 minutes on a high pressure using the 'Manual' mode. Once done, let the pressure naturally release. Then remove the cinnamon stick.
3. Fluff the salt, parsley, pepper on top of it and mix well. Enjoy!

Recipe # 57: Mixed Vegetable and Lentil Curry:

Serves: 6 people

Prep Time: 10 minutes

Cooking Time: 30 minutes

Ingredients:

1. 2 tablespoons of ghee
2. 1 teaspoon of cumin seeds
3. 1 tablespoon of Ginger
4. 1 carrot, peeled and sliced
5. 1/4 cup of green peas, frozen
6. 1/4 cup of green beans, chopped

7. 1 red potato, cubed
8. 1 tomato, diced
9. 1 cup of cabbage, chopped
10. 1 cup of cauliflower, chopped
11. 1 cup of spinach, chopped
12. 1/2 teaspoon of turmeric
13. 2 teaspoons of red chili powder
14. 2 teaspoon of salt
15. 1 cup of white rice
16. 1 cup of mixed lentils
17. 6 cups of water
18. 1/4 cup of cilantro, chopped for garnishing

Directions:

1. Preheat the Instant Pot using the 'Sauté' mode and add the ghee, cumin seeds and ginger. Cook it for 30 seconds, then add all the vegetables and mix properly. Add the turmeric, red chili powder, salt, rice ,the mixed lentils and stir properly.
2. Add 6 cups of water. Give everything a quick stir, and once done, cover the lid of the Instant Pot. Cook it for 12 minutes using the 'Rice' mode, and when the time is up, let the pressure naturally release.
3. Open the Instant Pot and transfer the curry to a large bowl. Garnish it with the cilantro and serve it hot with bread and pickles. Enjoy!

Recipe # 58: Not Re-Fried Beans:

Serves: 6 to 8 people

Prep Time: 5 minutes

Cooking Time: 10 minutes

Ingredients:

1. 1 tablespoon of oil
2. 1 onion, chopped
3. 1 bunch of cilantro, or parsley
4. 1/4 teaspoon of chipotle powder
5. 1/2 teaspoon of cumin
6. 2 cups borlotti of beans, dried
7. 2 cups of water
8. 1 teaspoon of salt

Directions:

1. Preheat the Instant Pot using the 'Sauté' mode. Add the oil, onions, cilantro stems, chipotle, cumin seeds and heat it until the onions begin to get softened.
2. Add the beans, water and cover the lid of the Instant Pot. Cook on a high pressure for 10 minutes using the 'Manual' mode. When the time is up, let the pressure naturally release.
3. Remove a heaping spoon of beans for garnishing, and sprinkle the rest in the cooker with salt. Mash the beans with a potato masher to the desired consistency.
4. Serve it with the sprinkled whole beans, parsley and some optional sour cream. Enjoy!

Recipe # 59: Chinese Steamed Eggs:

Serves: 2 people

Prep Time: 5 minutes

Cooking Time: 15 minutes

Ingredients:

1. 2 extra large eggs
2. 1 cup of chicken stock, homemade preferred

3. 1/4 teaspoon of sea salt
4. green onions, for garnishing
5. 1/2 tablespoon of light soy sauce
6. 1/2 tablespoon of fish sauce
7. 1 tablespoon of water

Directions:

1. Beat the eggs until the egg yolks and egg whites have fully been beaten. Then, add the chicken stock, sea salt and mix properly. Pour the mixture into another dish using a strainer, so that it will filter all the lumps produced in the process.
2. Tightly cover the dish with an aluminum foil. Don't forget to follow this step, or else the eggs will become crumble.
3. Place a trivet in the Instant Pot and pour 1 cup of water on it. Carefully place the egg dish into the trivet., cover the lid and cook for 6 minutes on a high pressure using the 'Manual' mode. When the time is up, let the pressure naturally release.
4. While the dish is cooking, make the soy sauce mixture by mixing the soy sauce, fish sauce and one tablespoon of water.
5. Open the lid and carefully remove the aluminum foil. Then garnish the dish with the green onions and pour the soy sauce mix over the eggs. Serve immediately and enjoy!

Recipe # 60: Quick Dry Beans:

Serves: 3 people

Prep Time: 1 minutes

Cooking Time: 2 minutes

Ingredients:

1. 1 cup of beans
2. 4 cups of water
3. 1 teaspoon of salt, optional

Directions:

1. Place the water, beans and salt into the Instant Pot. Cook for 2 to 8 minutes at a high pressure using the 'Manual' mode. Once the time is up, let the pressure naturally release.
2. Rinse and drain the beans, if you want to, you can add it to any recipe, or can eat it raw. Note that, if you want fewer amount of beans, you can reduce the ingredients of this recipe as much as you like, but ensure to keep the bean to a water ratio of 1:4. Enjoy!

Recipe # 61: Red Coconut Curry:

Serves: 4 people

Prep Time: 5 minutes

Cooking Time: 15 minutes

Ingredients:

1. 1 onion, diced
2. 3/4 cup of chickpeas, soaked overnight
3. 8 ounces' of white mushrooms, sliced
4. 2 garlic cloves, minced
5. 1 small green chili, diced
6. 1/2 tablespoon of turmeric, peeled
7. 1 tablespoon of ginger, peeled
8. 1 can of coconut milk
9. 1/2 cup of vegetable stock
10. 3 tablespoons of red curry paste

11. 1/2 tablespoon of salt
12. 1 teaspoon of cumin
13. 1/2 teaspoon of curry powder
14. 1/4 teaspoon of ground fenugreek
15. 1/4 teaspoon of black pepper
16. 1 tablespoon of tomato paste
17. 1 to 2 teaspoon of lemon juice
18. 1 cup of spinach

Directions:

1. Using the 'Sauté' mode of the Instant Pot, cook the mushrooms until they reduce in size, stirring every couple of minutes. Add the onions, stir and keep cooking until the onions are soft.
2. Add the garlic, chili, ginger, turmeric and heat it for 1 to 2 more minutes. Add all the remaining ingredients (except the tomato paste, lemon juice and spinach) into the Instant Pot and cover the lid.
3. Cook for 15 minutes on a high pressure using the 'Manual' mode. When the time is up, let the pressure naturally release. Then pour in the tomato paste, lemon juice, spinach and serve immediately. Enjoy!

Recipe # 62: Slow Cook Goat Cheese Lasagna:

Serves: 8 people

Prep Time: 15 minutes

Cooking Time: 2 hours

Ingredients:

1. 1 tablespoon of oil
2. 1 3/4 cups of onion, chopped
3. 1 cup of zucchini, diced

4. 1/2 cup of carrot, shredded
5. 2 cloves of garlic, chopped
6. 1/2 teaspoon of salt
7. 1/2 teaspoon of black pepper, freshly grounded
8. 1 can of tomatoes, crushed and undrained
9. Cooking spray
10. 1 cup of basil, fresh and chopped
11. 3/4 cup of part-skin ricotta cheese
12. 20 ounces' of spinach, frozen and chopped
13. 2 ounces' of goat cheese, roughly 1/4 cup
14. 8 gluten free lasagna noodles
15. 1-ounce of Parmesan cheese, about 1/4 cup
16. Basil leaves, optional

Directions:

1. Heat a 4-quart saucepan over an average pressure of heat. Add the oil to the pan, and then add the onion, zucchini and carrot. Cook for 5 minutes, then add the garlic, and stir for one more minute. Pour in the salt, pepper , tomatoes and simmer for 5 minutes.
2. Cover the inner pot of the Instant Pot with a cooking spray and mix the basil, ricotta, spinach and goat cheese in an average sized bowl. Spread 1/2 cup of spinach mix in the cooker, and arrange the noodles over the spinach mixture. Top the half of the remaining spinach mixture and 1 cup the tomato mixture.
3. Cover the lid of the Instant Pot and cook for 2 hours using the 'Slow Cook' mode. When the time is up, let the pressure naturally release. Top the dish with Parmesan cheese and basil leaves. Serve and Enjoy!

Recipe # 63: Smokey Sweet Black Eyed Peas:

Serves: 4 people

Prep Time: 5 minutes

Cooking Time: 20 minutes

Ingredients:

1. 1 tablespoon of oil
2. 1 onion, thinly sliced
3. 2 to 3 cloves of garlic, minced
4. 1 cup of red pepper, diced
5. 1 jalapeno, or any other hot chili
6. 1 to 2 teaspoons of smoked paprika
7. 1 to 2 teaspoons of chili powder
8. 1 1/2 cups of black eyed peas
9. 4 dates, chopped finely
10. 1 cup of water or vegetable broth
11. 1 can of fire roasted tomatoes
12. 2 cups of greens, chopped
13. salt, to taste

Directions:

1. Preheat the Instant Pot using the 'Sauté' mode. Dry heat the onions until they become translucent, adding water if required. Add the garlic, peppers and heat it for another minute. Add the smoked paprika and chili powder along with the peas and dates. Stir to coat them in the spice.
2. Add the water, stirring well to make sure that nothing sticks to the bottom of the pot. Close the lid, and cook at a high pressure for 3 minutes using the 'Manual' mode. Once the time is up and pressure has naturally released, carefully open the lid and add the tomatoes and greens.
3. Thereafter, lock the lid of the Instant Pot for 5 minutes, open it and add the salt to taste. Serve immediately and Enjoy!

Recipe # 64: Spice-rubbed Cauliflower Steaks:

Serves: 4 people

Prep Time: 10 minutes

Cooking Time: 5 minutes

Ingredients:

1. 1 large head cauliflower
2. 2 tablespoons of olive oil
3. 2 teaspoons of paprika
4. 2 teaspoons of ground cumin
5. 1 cup of cilantro, fresh and chopped
6. 1 lemon, quartered

Directions:

1. Insert the steam rack into the Instant Pot. Add 1 and a 1/2 cups of water. Remove the leaves from the cauliflower and trim the core so that it sits flat. Thereafter, place it into the steam rack.
2. Using a small bowl, mix the olive oil, paprika, cumin and salt. Drizzle it over the cauliflower and rub it to coat. Cover the lid and cook on a high pressure for 4 minutes using the 'Manual' mode.
3. When the time is up, do a quick pressure release. Lift the cauliflower onto a cutting board and slice it into a 1 inch of steak. Divide it among the plates and sprinkle it with the cilantro. Serve it with the lemon quarters and Enjoy!

Recipe # 65: Spicy Sous-Vide Tempeh:

Serves: 4 people

Prep Time: 15 minutes

Cooking Time: 3 hours

Ingredients:

1. 1 package tempeh
2. 1/4 cup of brown rice syrup
3. 2 tablespoons of chili paste
4. 1 tablespoon of red miso paste
5. 1 teaspoon of rice vinegar
6. 1 teaspoon of sesame seeds
7. 1 teaspoon of olive or canola oil

Directions:

1. Set the sous vide to 190 degree Fahrenheit using the Instant Pot, for 3 hours. While the sous vide is preheating, mix the brown rice syrup, chili paste, red miso paste, rice vinegar and the sesame seeds in a bowl.
2. Place the entire block of the tempeh in a bag, and scrape the sauce in a bag. Seal the bag and place it in a container. Once the sous vide has heated, cook for 3 hours using the 'Manual' mode.
3. Serve immediately. Enjoy!

Recipe # 66: Shrimp and Grits:

Serves: 4 people

Prep Time: 5 minutes

Cooking Time: 45 minutes

Ingredients:

1. 1-pound of shrimp, deveined
2. 2 teaspoons of old bay seasoning
3. 3 strips if smoked bacon, diced
4. 1/3 cup of onion, chopped finely
5. 1/2 cup of bell peppers, red or green
6. 1 tablespoon of garlic, minced
7. 2 tablespoons of dry white wine
8. 1 1/2 cups of tomatoes, diced
9. 2 tablespoons of lemon juice
10. 1/4 cup of chicken broth
11. 1/4 teaspoon of Tabasco sauce
12. 1/2 teaspoon of salt
13. 1/4 teaspoon of black pepper
14. 1/4 cup of heavy cream
15. 1/4 cup of scallions, thinly sliced
16. 1/2 cup of grits, for grits
17. 1 cup of milk, for grits
18. 1 cup of water, for grits
19. salt, for grits, to taste
20. pepper, for grits, to taste
21. 1 tablespoon of butter, for grits

Directions:

1. Dry the shrimp, sprinkle it with the seasoning and set it aside.Using the 'Sauté' mode, cook the bacon until it gets crisp and brown, at about 4 minutes. Remove it to a plate and set aside.
2. Heat the onions and bell peppers in the bacon fat, at about 2 to 3 minutes. Add the garlic and heat it briefly. Turn the Instant Pot off, deglaze it with the white wine and stir properly to to remove any browned bits.
3. Pour in the tomatoes, lemon juice, broth, hot sauce, salt and pepper. Place the trivet in the Instant Pot. In a medium bowl that fits into the Instant Pot, stir together all the grit ingredients. Place the bowl in the trivet.
4. Close the Instant Pot lid, and cook for 10 minutes on a high pressure using the 'Manual' mode. Once done, allow the pressure to release naturally. Open the

Instant Pot, remove the grits and set it aside.

5. Remove the trivet and carefully stir in the shrimp. Close the Pot immediately and let the shrimp cook in the residual heat. After 10 minutes, open the Instant Pot and gently stir the shrimp while adding the cream.
6. Garnish it with the scallions and bacon. Serve the grits topped with shrimp and sauce. Enjoy!

Recipe # 67: Mussels with Red Pepper Garlic Sauce:

Serves: 4 people

Prep Time: 15 minutes

Cooking Time: 1 minutes

Ingredients:

1. 1 tablespoon of olive oil
2. 3 pounds of mussels
3. 4 cloves of garlic, minced
4. 1 large red bell pepper, minced
5. 3/4 cup fish stock, clam juice
6. 1/2 cup dry white wine
7. 1/8 teaspoon of red pepper flakes
8. 2 tablespoons of cream, whipping
9. 3 tablespoon of parsley, chopped

Directions:

1. Clean the mussels, preheat the Instant Pot using the 'Sauté' mode, heat the olive oil until it simmers. Thereafter, add the garlic and stir until it produces fragrance. Add the roasted red pepper,, fish stock, wine and the red pepper flakes. Then stir well and combine evenly.
2. Add the mussels to the pot, cover the lid and cook for 1 minute on a high

pressure using the 'Manual' mode. When done, do a quick pressure release.
3. Stir in the heavy cream, parsley and serve with cooking liquid. Enjoy!

Recipe # 68: New England Clam Chowder:

Serves: 4 to 6 people

Prep Time: 5 minutes

Cooking Time: 10 minutes

Ingredients:

1. 300 grams' of clams, strained and frozen
2. 2 cups of clam juice
3. 1 cup of bacon, smoked and cured
4. 1 onion, finely chopped
5. 1/2 cup of white wine
6. 2 potatoes, cubed
7. 1 bay leaf
8. 1 sprig thyme
9. 1 pinch of cayenne pepper
10. 1 cup of milk
11. 1 cup of cream
12. 1 teaspoon of butter, melted
13. 1 tablespoon of flour

Directions:

1. Add the cubed bacon to the Instant Pot, and heat it until the bacon begins to sizzle. Add the onion, salt, pepper and raise the heat of the Instant Pot.
2. Once the onions have softened, deglaze using wine and scrape the brown bits on the bottom of the pot. Let the wine evaporate and then add the diced potatoes, clam juice, bay leaf, thyme and the cayenne pepper.

3. Cover the lid and cook for 5 minutes on a high pressure using the 'Manual; mode. While it is cooking, make a roux to thicken the chowder by blending equal amounts of butter and flour over a low heat and stir constantly until they are well blended.
4. When the time is up, do a quick pressure release. Add the roux, milk, cream and clams. Change the mode to the Sauté and simmer all the ingredients for about 5 minutes or so.
5. Serve it with soup crackers or in a fresh bread bowl. Enjoy!

Recipe # 69: Coconut Fish Curry:

Serves: 4 people

Prep Time: 5 minutes

Cooking Time: 20 minutes

Ingredients:

1. 1 1/2 pounds' of white fish fillet
2. 1 heaping cup of cherry tomatoes
3. 2 green chilies, sliced into strips
4. 2 medium onions, sliced into strips
5. 2 cloves of garlic, chopped
6. 1 tablespoon of ginger, freshly grated
7. 6 curry leaves, or bay or basil leaves
8. 1 tablespoon of ground coriander
9. 1 tablespoon of ground cumin
10. 1/2 teaspoon of ground turmeric
11. 1 teaspoon of chili powder
12. 1/2 teaspoon of grounded fenugreek
13. 2 cups of coconut milk, unsweetened
14. salt, to taste

15. lemon juice, to taste

Directions:

1. Using the 'Sauté' mode in the Instant Pot, add the oil and curry leaves. Lightly fry it until they are golden around the edges, at about 1 minute. Then, add the onion, garlic, ginger and heat it until the onion is soft.
2. Add all the ground spice, heat them together until they have released their aroma, at about one minute. Then, deglaze the pot with the coconut milk, scraping everything from the bottom of the pot to add into the sauce. After that, add in the green chilies, tomatoes fish and Stir to coat properly.
3. Close the lid of the Instant Pot, and cook for 3 minutes on a high pressure using the 'Manual' mode. When the time is up, do a quick pressure release.
4. Add the salt and lemon juice to taste before serving. Enjoy!

Recipe # 70: Seafood Stew:

Serves: 4 to 6 people

Prep Time: 10 minutes

Cooking Time: 10 minutes

Ingredients:

1. 3 tablespoons of extra-virgin olive oil
2. 2 bay leaves
3. 2 teaspoons of paprika
4. a small onion, thinly sliced
5. 1 small green bell pepper, thinly sliced
6. 1 1/2 cups of tomatoes, diced
7. 2 cloves of garlic, smashed
8. sea salt, to taste
9. pepper, grounded, to taste

10. 1 cup of fish stock
11. 1 1/2 pounds' of meaty fish, 2 inch chunks
12. 1-pound of shrimp, cleaned and deveined
13. 12 little neck clams
14. 1/4 cup of cilantro, for garnishing
15. 1 tablespoon of olive oil, for serving

Directions:

1. Using the 'Sauté' mode on the Instant Pot, add the olive oil, bay leaves, and the paprika. Stir it for 30 seconds and then add the onion, bell pepper, tomatoes, garlic, 2 tablespoons of cilantro, salt and pepper. Thereafter, stir it for a few minutes.
2. Add fish stock and water. Season the fish with salt and pepper. Nestle the clams and shrimps among the veggies in the Instant Pot. Add fish pieces to the top.
3. Close the lid tightly, and using the 'Manual' mode of the Instant Pot, cook for 10 minutes on high pressure. Once done, let the pressure naturally release.
4. Divide the stew among bowls. Drizzle with extra olive oil and sprinkle the excess cilantro and serve immediately. Enjoy!

Side Dishes:

Recipe # 71: 1 minute Peruvian Quinoa:

Serves: 4 to 6 people

Prep Time: 1 minute

Cooking Time: 1 minute

Ingredients:

1. 1 cup of quinoa, rinsed well
2. 1 pinch of salt, or more if desired
3. 1 1/2 cups of water
4. 1 lime, squeezed and zested

Directions:

1. In the Instant Pot, add the quinoa, salt, lime, and water. Cover the lid, let it cook for 1 minute on a high pressure 'Manual' mode and when it is done, let the pressure naturally release.
2. Mix with lime juice and season it with any additional salt. Serve with seasonal veggies. Enjoy!

Recipe # 72: Instant Cheese Sauce:

Serves: 4 to 5 people

Prep Time: 5 minutes

Cooking Time: 5 minutes

Ingredients:

1. 2 cup of potatoes, peeled and chopped
2. 1 cup of carrot, chopped

3. 1/2 cup of yellow onion, chopped
4. 3 cloves of garlic, peeled and left whole
5. 1/2 cup of nutritional yeast
6. 1/2 cup of raw cashews
7. 1 teaspoon of turmeric
8. 1 teaspoon of salt
9. 2 cups of water

Directions:

1. Place all the ingredients in the Instant Pot, then cook for 5 minutes on a high pressure using the 'Manual' mode. Once done, do a quick pressure release and transfer all the mixture to a blender, then blend until it gets creamy.
2. Serve it with pasta, vegetables or as a dip. Enjoy!

Recipe # 73: Bulgar Pilaf:

Serves: 4 to 6 people

Prep Time: 6 minutes

Cooking Time: 12 minutes

Ingredients:

1. 1 tablespoon of olive oil
2. 1 tablespoon of butter
3. 3 tablespoons of onion, finely chopped
4. 1 cup of a medium sized bulgur wheat
5. 2 cups of chicken broth
6. 1/2 teaspoon of table salt
7. 1/2 teaspoon of Italian seasoning
8. lime wedges, for garnishing
9. chopped cashews, for garnishing

Directions:

1. Add the olive oil, butter into the Instant Pot and using the 'Sauté' mode, cook it until the butter melts. Add the onion, celery while cooking and stirring constantly for 2 minutes. Add the bulger, chicken broth and Italian seasoning.
2. Secure the lid and change the mode to 'Rice'. Cook on a low pressure for 12 minutes and once it is done, do a quick pressure release.
3. Remove the lid, fluff pilaf with a fork and garnish it with lime wedges and chopped cashews. Enjoy!

Recipe # 74: Cherry and Farro Salad:

Serves: 6 to 8 people

Prep Time: 10 minutes

Cooking Time: 40 minutes

Ingredients:

1. 1 cup of whole grain Farro
2. 1 tablespoon of apple cidar vinegar
3. 1 teaspoon of lemon juice
4. 1 tablespoon of olive oil
5. 1/4 teaspoon of sea salt
6. 1/2 cup of dried cherries
7. 1/4 cup of chives, or green onions, finely minced
8. 8 to 10 leaves mint, minced
9. 2 cups of cherries, cut in half

Directions:

1. Add 3 cups of Farro into the Instant Pot and cook on a high pressure for 40 minutes using the 'Manual' mode. Once done, do a quick pressure release.
2. Drain the Farro, and put it into a bowl. Mix it with the vinegar, lemon juice,

oil, salt, dried cherries, chives and mint. Thereafter, refrigerate it until it gets cold.

3. Before serving, pour in the fresh berries. Enjoy!

Recipe # 75: Classic Mashed Potatoes:

Serves: 4 to 8 people

Prep Time: 2 minutes

Cooking Time: 20 minutes

Ingredients:

1. 5 to 8 potatoes
2. 2 cups of water
3. 1 teaspoon of salt
4. 1/3 cup of cream
5. salt and pepper, to taste

Directions:

1. Add the potatoes, water and salt into the Instant Pot. Cover the lid and cook it for 20 minutes on a high pressure using the 'Manual' mode.
2. Once done, transfer the potatoes into a mixing bowl, remove the skins and clean it thoroughly. Add 2 tablespoons of the cooking liquid, two of the cream and start mashing with a potato masher.
3. Keep mashing while adding small quantities of the liquid and cream just until you reach the desired state. Thereafter, add the salt and pepper to taste. Serve and enjoy!

Recipe # 76: Creamy Mashed Sweet Potatoes:

Serves: 2 to 4 people

Prep Time: 5 minutes

Cooking Time: 20 minutes

Ingredients:

1. 2 pounds of sweet potatoes, cut into 1 inch chunks
2. 2 to 3 tablespoons of butter
3. 2 tablespoons of maple syrup
4. 1/4 teaspoon of nutmeg
5. 1 cup of cold water
6. sea salt, to taste

Directions:

1. Pour the cold water and potato chunks into the Instant Pot. Cover the lid and cook on a high pressure for 8 minutes using the 'Manual' mode. Once done, do a quick pressure release.
2. Place the cooked sweet potatoes into a large bowl and mash them partially. Add the nutmeg, butter, maple syrup and keep mashing until you reach your desired look.
3. Season it with the salt to enhance the flavors. Serve and Enjoy!

Recipe # 77: Garlic and Chive Mashed Potatoes:

Serves: 5 people

Prep Time: 8minutes

Cooking Time: 9 minutes

Ingredients:

1. 2 cups of chicken stock
2. 2 pounds of peeled Yukon potatoes
3. 4 cloves garlic, peeled
4. 1 cup of plain Greek yogurt
5. 1/2 cup of whole milk
6. 1/2 teaspoon of salt
7. 1/4 cup of chives, freshly chopped

Directions:

1. Mix the broth, potatoes, garlic into the Instant Pot and cook on a high pressure for 9 minutes using the 'Manual' setting. Once done, do a quick pressure release.
2. Mash the potato with a potato masher until you reach the desired state. Pour in the milk, salt and yogurt. Thereafter, add the chives just before serving. Enjoy!

Recipe # 78: Instant Roasted Potatoes:

Serves: 4 to 6 people

Prep Time: 1 minute

Cooking Time: 24 minutes

Ingredients:

1. 4 to 8 potatoes
2. 2 tablespoons of olive oil
3. kosher salt, to taste
4. black pepper, to taste

Directions:

1. Clean the potatoes, and makes small holes using a fork. Add one cup of cold

water and the potatoes into the Instant Pot. Cover the lid and cook on a high pressure for 12 minutes using the 'Manual' mode.

2. Serve the piping hot with butter, kosher salt and the grounded black pepper. Serve and Enjoy!

Recipe # 79: Lemony English Peas:

Serves: 4 to 6 people

Prep Time: 1 minute

Cooking Time: 3 minutes

Ingredients:

1. 1 to 2 cloves of garlic, minced
2. 2 cups of English peas, fresh or frozen
3. 2 cups of asparagus, cut into 2 inch pieces
4. 1/2 cup of vegetable broth
5. 1 lemon, juiced and zested
6. 2 to 3 tablespoons of pine nuts, toasted

Directions:

1. Add the garlic, peas, asparagus and the vegetable broth into the Instant Pot. Cook on a low pressure for 2 minutes using the 'Manual' mode.
2. Add the lemon zest, juice and stir. Then transfer it to a large bowl and garnish it with the pine nuts. Enjoy!

Recipe # 80: Maple Glazed Carrots:

Serves: 4 people

Prep Time: 5 minutes

Cooking Time: 4 minutes

Ingredients:

1. 2 pounds' of carrots, peeled and thickly sliced
2. 1/4 cup of raisins
3. 1 cup of water
4. 1 tablespoon of maple syrup
5. 1 tablespoon of butter
6. pepper, to taste

Directions:

1. Put the carrots, raisins and the water into the Instant Pot, then cook for 4 minutes on a high pressure using the 'Manual' mode. Once the time is up, do a quick release of the pressure through the valve.
2. Strain the carrots, while the carrots are straining, melt the butter and maple the syrup into the Instant Pot.
3. Mix properly, tumble in the carrots,raisins and coat it with butter and sauce. Serve with freshly grounded pepper. Enjoy!

Recipe # 81: Mexican Polenta:

Serves: 3 to 6 people

Prep Time: 5 minutes

Cooking Time: 15 minutes

Ingredients:

1. 1 cup of green onion, sliced
2. 2 teaspoons of garlic, minced
3. 2 cups of vegetable broth
4. 2 cups of boiling water
5. 1 cup of corn meal, grits
6. 1/4 cups of cilantro, fresh and chopped
7. 1 tablespoon of chili powder
8. 1 teaspoon of cumin
9. 1 teaspoon of oregano
10. 1/2 teaspoon of smoked paprika
11. 1/4 teaspoon of cayenne pepper

Directions:

1. Using the 'Sauté' mode in the Instant Pot, heat the green onion and the minced garlic until it produces some fragrance, while only adding a small amount of water. Then,pour in the vegetable broth, water, corn meal, cilantro, spices and stir to mix properly.
2. Cover the lid and cook on a high pressure for 5 minutes using the 'Manual' mode. Once done, do a quick pressure release. Serve as it is, or place it in a glass dish alongside with other recipes. Enjoy!

Recipe # 82: One Pot Brussels Sprouts:

Serves: 4 to 6 people

Prep Time: 10 minutes

Cooking Time: 20 minutes

Ingredients:

1. 5 slices of bacon, chopped
2. 6 cups of Brussel sprouts, chopped

3. 1/4 teaspoon of salt
4. 2 tablespoons of water
5. 2 tablespoons of balsamic reduction
6. 1/4 cup of goat cheese, optional
7. pepper, to taste

Directions:

1. Using the 'Sauté' mode of the Instant Pot, add the chopped bacon. Heat it until the desired crispiness is reached. Thereafter, add the chopped Brussel sprouts and stir to cover with the flavorful bacon fat.
2. Add the water and sprinkle it with salt and pepper. Then cover it, stir, every few minutes and replace the lid. Then continue to heat it uncovered until the Brussels crisps up.
3. Transfer it to a serving dish, top it with the balsamic reduction and goat cheese. Enjoy!

Recipe # 83: Perfect Mashed Potatoes and Parsnips:

Serves: 6 people

Prep Time: 5 minutes

Cooking Time: 12 minutes

Ingredients:

1. 3 pounds of Yukon gold potatoes, peeled and cut into 1 1/2 inch cubes
2. 1 pound of parsnips, cut into 1-inch-thick circles
3. 1 teaspoon of pepper
4. 1 teaspoon of salt
5. 4 tablespoons of butter, room temperature
6. 4 tablespoons of half-and-half

Directions:

1. Pour 2 cups of water into the inner pot of the Instant Pot. Place the steamer basket in the pot, add the potatoes and parsnips into it.
2. Cover the Instant Pot's lid and cook on a high pressure for 7 minutes using the 'Manual' mode. Once the time is up, do a quick pressure release.
3. Open the Instant Pot and remove the steamer basket. Sprinkle it with salt and pepper. Using a potato masher, mash the potatoes and the parsnips, thereafter add the butter and half-and-half. Then mix properly.
4. Garnish it with the fresh herbs if desired. Enjoy!

Recipe # 84: Cranberry Sauce:

Serves: 3 people

Prep Time: 5 minutes

Cooking Time: 15 minutes

Ingredients:

1. 12 ounces' of cranberries, rinsed and stems removed
2. 2 1/2 teaspoons of orange zest
3. 1/4 cup of orange juice, freshly squeezed
4. 2 tablespoons of maple syrup, or honey
5. pinch of salt
6. 1/2 to 1 cup of white sugar

Directions:

1. Mix the maple syrup, orange juice and pour it into the Instant Pot. Add the lemon zest, 10 ounces' of cranberries and reserve the other 2 ounces for later use.
2. Close the lid and cook on a high pressure for 1 minutes using the 'Manual' mode. Once done, let the pressure naturally release for 7 minutes.
3. Switch the mode to 'sauté' and break the cranberries with a spoon. Then, add

the white sugar, the remaining cranberries and stir. By that time,the heat will instantly melt the sugar to form a thick cranberry sauce, which will require you to add a pinch of salt.

4. Serve hot or cold with your favorite dish. Enjoy!

Recipe # 85: Hard-Boiled Eggs:

Serves: 3 to 6 people

Prep Time: 1 minutes

Cooking Time: 5 minutes

Ingredients:

1. 1 to 6 eggs
2. 1 cup of water, cold only
3. Salt and pepper, to taste

Directions:

1. Fill the Instant Pot with one cup of cold water. Place the eggs, lock the lid and cook for 5 minutes on a high pressure using the 'Manual' mode. When the time is up, do a quick pressure release.
2. Place the the eggs into a container filled with cold water. Keep the water cool by consistently adding more water from the sink. If you want to serve it warm, cool it for 1 minute and if cold, then cool it off for 3 minutes.
3. Tap the 2 ends and the middle of the egg to peel delicately, then sprinkle the pepper and salt on top it. Serve it with other morning food and enjoy!

Recipe # 86: Red, White and Green Brussel Sprouts:

Serves: 4 people

Prep Time: 10 minutes

Cooking Time: 3 minutes

Ingredients:

1. 1 pound of Brussel Sprouts
2. 1/4 cup of pine nuts, toasted
3. 1 pomegranate
4. 1 tablespoon of extra-virgin olive oil
5. 1/2 teaspoon
6. 1 grate pepper

Directions:

1. Remove the leaves, stems, of the Brussel Sprouts and cut the large ones in half so that all of them will be of equal size. Prepare the Instant Pot by pouring one cup of water and adding a steamer basket. Thereafter, put the sprouts in the basket.
2. Cover the lid and cook for 3 minutes on a high pressure using the 'Manual' mode. When the time is up, let the pressure naturally release.
3. Move the sprouts into a dish and dress in the olive oil, salt and pepper prior to sprinkling toasted pine nuts and the pomegranate seeds. Serve at a room temperature. Enjoy!

Recipe # 87: Roasted Baby Potatoes:

Serves: 4 to 6 people

Prep Time: 1 minute

Cooking Time: 20 minutes

Ingredients:

1. 5 tablespoons of vegetable oil
2. 2 pounds of fingerling potatoes, or small baby potatoes
3. 1 sprig rosemary
4. 3 cloves of garlic
5. 1 cup of stock
6. salt, to taste
7. pepper, to taste

Directions:

1. Preheat the Instant Pot using the 'sauté' mode, and add the potatoes, garlic and rosemary. Roll the potatoes around to cook them on both sides.
2. Using a knife, pierce the potatoes in the middle. Pour in the stock and cover the lid. Cook it on a high pressure for 11 minutes using the 'Manual' mode. Once done, quickly release the pressure.
3. Remove the outer skin of the cloves and serve it wholely or mashed with the potatoes. Then, sprinkle the salt and pepper on top of it. Enjoy!

Recipe # 88: Smokey Sweet Potato Mash:

Serves: 4 people

Prep Time: 10 minutes

Cooking Time: 11 minutes

Ingredients:

1. 1 cup of water
2. 3 medium sized sweet potatoes, scrubbed
3. 1/4 cup of butter

4. 1/4 cup l of light brown sugar, packed
5. 1/2 teaspoon of smoked paprika
6. 1/4 teaspoon of table salt
7. 4 bacon sliced, cooked and crumbled

Directions:

1. Place the steam rack into the Instant Pot and pour in some water. Place the potatoes in the rack. And cover the lid while cooking on a high pressure for 11 to 14 minutes using the 'Manual' mode. Once done, do a quick pressure release.
2. When it gets cool enough, peel the potatoes and place it in a large bowl. Mash it roughly and pour in the butter, sugar, salt and paprika. Thereafter, sprinkle it with the crumbled bacon and serve immediately. Enjoy!

Recipe # 89: Thick Nacho Cheese Sauce:

Serves: 4 people

Prep Time: 10 minutes

Cooking Time: 15 minutes

Ingredients:

1. 2 cups of potatoes, cubed
2. 1 cup of yellow onion, chopped
3. 1 cup of carrot, chopped
4. 1/2 jar roasted red bell peppers
5. 1/2 cup of cashews
6. 2 cups of water
7. 1/3 cup of nutritional yeast
8. 1 tablespoon of Dijon mustard
9. 2 teaspoons of lemon juice

10. 1 teaspoon of salt
11. 1/4 teaspoon of liquid smoke

Directions:

1. Add the potatoes, onions, carrots, cashews, and water into the Instant Pot. Cover the lid and while using the 'Manual' mode, cook for 2 minutes at a high pressure. Once done, let the pressure naturally release.
2. Using a spoon, transfer the vegetable mixture and liquid to a blender. Add the nutritional yeast, mustard, lemon juice, salt, liquid smoke and blend until it gets smooth and creamy. Serve and enjoy!

Recipe # 90: Corn on the Cob:

Serves: 4 people

Prep Time: 5 minutes

Cooking Time: 20 minutes

Ingredients:

1. 4 ears corn, on the cob
2. 3 tablespoons of light soy sauce
3. 2 tablespoons of shacha sauce
4. 1 tablespoon of sugar
5. 1 teaspoon of garlic powder
6. 1/4 teaspoon of sesame oil

Directions:

1. Pour 1 cup of cold tap water into the Instant Pot, place a trivet into the pressure cooker and keep the corn in the trivet. Cover the lid and cook at a 'Manual' mode on a high pressure for 2 minutes. Once done, do a quick pressure release.
2. While the corn is cooking in the Instant Pot, preheat the oven to 450 degrees

Fahrenheit. Mix the light soy sauce, shacha sauce, sugar, garlic powder, and 1/4 teaspoon of sesame oil in a small mixing bowl.

3. Then brush the sauce on the corn on all sides using a brush and place them on a baking tray in the oven for 5 to 10 minutes. Serve immediately and enjoy!

Recipe # 91: Carrot Puree:

Serves: 2 to 4 people

Prep Time: 5 minutes

Cooking Time: 4 minutes

Ingredients:

1. 1 1/2 pounds' of carrots, roughly chopped
2. 1 tablespoon of butter, room temperature
3. 1 tablespoon of honey
4. 1/4 teaspoon of sea salt
5. 1 cup of water

Directions:

1. Pour the water into the Instant Pot, and add the carrots into it. Cook for 4 minutes on a high pressure using the 'Manual' mode with the lid covered. Once done, quick release the pressure.
2. Place the carrots in a deep bowl, use a hand blender to blend the carrots until they reach the desired state. Then add butter, honey and sea salt to the puree, then mix properly.
3. Taste the carrot puree, and add the brown sugar for more sweetness if necessary. Serve immediately with the main dish. Enjoy!

Recipe # 92: Paleo Beet Borscht:

Serves: 4 people

Prep Time: 20 minutes

Cooking Time: 45 minutes

Ingredients:

1. 8 cups of beets
2. ½ cup of celery, diced
3. ½ cup of carrots, diced
4. 2 cloves of garlic, diced
5. 1 medium sized onion, diced
6. 3 cups of cabbage, shredded
7. 6 cups of stock, beef or chicken
8. 1 bay leaf
9. 1 tablespoon of salt
10. ½ tablespoons of thyme
11. ½ cup of dill, freshly chopped
12. ½ cup of coconut yogurt, plain

Directions:

1. Place the beets in the Instant Pot with 1 cup of water. Steam it for 7 minutes, then quick release the pressure. Drop it straight into ice cold water, as the skins will peel off by themselves.
2. Put the beets, carrots, garlic, celery, onions, bay leaf, cabbage, salt, stock and the thyme into the Instant Pot, then cook for 45 minutes using the 'Soup' mode.
3. When the time is up, allow a natural release so that the soup won't splatter.
4. Scoop the Beet Borscht into bowls, and add some dairy free yogurt. Garnish it with the fresh dill. Enjoy!

Recipe # 93: Instant Mexi-Cali Rice:

Serves: 4 to 6 people

Prep Time: 5 minutes

Cooking Time: 5 minutes

Ingredients:

1. 6 cups of brown rice, cooked
2. 1 can of Fire Roasted Tomatoes
3. 2 cups of salsa, homemade or branded
4. 4 tablespoons of tomato paste
5. 3 cups of onion, chopped
6. 6 cloves of garlic, finely minced
7. 1 1/2 cup of water

Directions:

1. Place all the ingredients in the Instant Pot, and cook on a high pressure for 5 minutes. When the time is up, do a quick pressure release.
2. You can pour in some chopped cilantro if you like or garnish it with any type of topping you like. Enjoy!

Recipe # 94: Butternut Squash Risotto:

Serves: 6 to 8 people

Prep Time: 21 minutes

Cooking Time: 12 minutes

Ingredients:

1. 2 teaspoons of olive oil

2. 1/2 cup of yellow onion, chopped
3. 1 1/2 cups of Arborio rice
4. 1 cup of water
5. 1/2 teaspoon of table salt
6. 1/4 teaspoon of black pepper, grounded
7. 3 cups of butternut squash, 3/4 inch pieces
8. 2 cans of beef broth
9. 1/2 cup of Parmigiano-Reggiano cheese
10. 3 tablespoons of unsalted butter
11. 2 tablespoons of fresh parsley, finely chopped

Directions:

1. Preheat the Instant Pot using the 'Sauté' mode, and add the oil. Thereafter add the onion and cook for 5 minutes. Then, add the rice, and cook for 1 more minute until the rice is covered with the oil.
2. Add 1/2 cup of water, salt and pepper, cook it until the water is absorbed and cover the lid, using the 'Rice' mode, on a low pressure for 12 minutes.
3. When the time is up, do a quick pressure release. Add the cheese, butter and the parsley, while still stirring until it gets creamy. Serve immediately.

Recipe # 95: Chicken and Pancetta Risotto:

Serves: 4 people

Prep Time: 10 minutes

Cooking Time: 12 minutes

Ingredients:

1. 2 cloves of garlic, chopped
2. 100 grams' of butter
3. 1 tablespoon of olive oil

4. salt and pepper, to taste
5. 50 grams' of pancetta, diced
6. 300 grams' of chicken, diced
7. 300 grams of Arborio rice
8. 4 tablespoons of parmesan, grated
9. 1/3 cup of white wine
10. 3 1/4 cups of chicken stock
11. 1 tablespoon of fresh thyme
12. lemon zest, for garnishing
13. basil leaves, for garnishing

Directions:

1. Using the 'Sauté' mode of the Instant Pot, add the oil and 30 grams of butter. Heat the onion, garlic, pancetta and chicken for 2 minutes.
2. Pour in rice, add the time and stir in the wine. Empty in the stock and stir really properly. Using the 'Manual' mode, cook on a high pressure for 12 minutes.
3. At the end of the time, quick release the pressure. Stir the risotto well to form a creamy texture and pour in the grated Parmesan. Then, leave it to stand for 3 minutes.
4. Serve the topped with an extra Parmesan, freshly grounded pepper, grated lemon zest and the basil leaves. Enjoy!

Recipe # 96: Confetti Basmati Rice:

Serves: 4 to 6 people

Prep Time: 5 minutes

Cooking Time: 5 minutes

Ingredients:

1. 1 tablespoon of olive oil
2. 1 medium sized onion, chopped
3. 1 bell pepper, any color
4. 1 carrot, grated
5. water, as needed in the recipe directions
6. 2 cups of basmati rice, or long-grain rice
7. 1/2 cup of peas, frozen
8. 1 teaspoon of salt

Directions:

1. Preheat the Instant Pot using the 'Sauté' mode. Add the oil, onion and heat it until it becomes translucent. In the meantime, using a 4 cup capacity liquid container, add the bell pepper, grated carrots and pat lightly into an even layer.
2. Pour the water into the container until all the ingredients reach the 3 cup mark and set it aside. Back to the Instant Pot, pour in the rice, peas, salt and mix properly.
3. Add the measuring cup with the water and veggies into the Instant Pot and cover the lid. Cook it for 3 minutes on a high pressure using the 'Manual' mode.
4. When the time is up, let the pressure naturally release, fluff the rice with a fork, serve and enjoy!

Recipe # 97: Fluffy Jasmine Rice:

Serves: 4 people

Prep Time: 1 minute

Cooking Time: 15 minutes

Ingredients:

1. 2 1/2 cup of water
2. 2 cup of Jasmine rice
3. 1/2 teaspoon of sea salt, optional

Directions:

1. Add the water, rice , salt, the Instant Pot and cover ie with a glass lid. Then, using the 'Sauté' mode, boil the water.
2. Now press the 'Keep Warm/Cancel' twice to cancel the sauté mode and activate the keep warm mode. Use the keep warm timer for 9 minutes, and after that,, cancel the keep warm mode.
3. Fluff the rice with a fork before serving. Enjoy!

Recipe # 98: Perfect Brown Rice:

Serves: 4 people

Prep Time: 1 minute

Cooking Time: 22 minutes

Ingredients:

1. 2 cups of brown rice
2. 2 1/2 cups of water

Directions:

1. Add the rice, water to the Instant Pot and secure the lid. Cook on a 'Manual' mode for 22 minutes on a high pressure. When the time is up, let the pressure naturally release.
2. Serve alongside your favorite main dishes. Enjoy!

Recipe # 99: Pasta Caprese:

Serves: 3 people

Prep Time: 5 minutes

Cooking Time: 10 minutes

Ingredients:

1. 2 1/2 cups of mezze penne
2. 1 onion, thinly sliced
3. 1 tablespoon of olive oil
4. 1 can of tomato sauce
5. 6 garlic cloves, minced
6. 1 cup of grape tomatoes, halved
7. 4 handfuls basil leaves
8. ¼ cup of balsamic vinegar
9. 1 teaspoon salt
10. 1 teaspoon of red pepper, optional
11. Parmesan Cheese, optional
12. 1 cup of mozzarella balls, fresh
13. 1 cup of water

Directions:

1. Adjust the Instant Pot to 'the Sauté' mode and add the onion, oil, garlic and red pepper. Heat it for one minute, then add the grape tomatoes, pasta, pasta sauce, half of the basil leaves, water and stir evenly.
2. Seal the lid of the Instant Pot and cook on a high pressure for 4 minutes using the 'Manual' setting. Once done, do a quick pressure release, add the mozzarella cheese and vinegar.
3. Serve it hot and garnish it with the chopped basil and shredded Parmesan. Enjoy!

Recipe # 100: Macaroni and Cheese:

Serves: 8 people

Prep Time: 5 minutes

Cooking Time: 6 minutes

Ingredients:

1. 1-pound of elbow macaroni
2. 4 cups of chicken broth
3. 12 ounces' of Cheddar Cheese, shredded
4. 3 tablespoons of unsalted butter
5. ½ cup of Parmesan Cheese, shredded
6. ½ cup of sour cream
7. 1/8 teaspoon of cayenne pepper
8. 1 ½ teaspoons of yellow mustard

Directions:

1. Mix the macaroni, broth and butter into the Instant Pot. Cover the lid and cook it on a high pressure for 6 minutes using the 'Manual' mode. Once done, do a quick pressure release.
2. Open the pot and pour in the cheeses, sour cream, cayenne pepper and mustard. Let the mixture thicken for 5 minutes, then serve. Enjoy!

Recipe # 101: Minestrone Soup:

Serves: 4 to 6 people

Prep Time: 5 minutes

Cooking Time: 20 minutes

Ingredients:

1. 1 cup of beans, cooked
2. 1-pound of ground beef, browned
3. 1 potato, diced
4. 2 carrots, diced
5. 2 stalks celery, diced
6. 1 onion
7. 2 cloves of garlic
8. 32 ounces' of chicken broth
9. 28 ounces' of tomatoes, crushed
10. 2 teaspoon of tomato paste
11. 2 tablespoon of Italian Seasoning
12. 1 teaspoon of salt

Directions:

1. Mix all the ingredients in the Instant Pot and close the lid. Cook at a 'Manual' mode for 20 minutes on a high pressure. Once done, let the pressure naturally release for 10 minutes, then do a quick release.
2. Serve and enjoy!

The Final Words

Hope you like this small, but helpful cookbook for a topic not discussed in the food category too often. A instant pot is definitely a great addition to the everyday kitchen arsenal of both men and women, and taking the health benefits into note, you can say that it is the best choice for a cooking appliance! So, if you have a instant pot and an empty stomach, go ahead and try a recipe out today!

Thanks for buying this book, your support is what keeps me going!